D0297241

MEASURING BUSINESS PERFORMANCE

OTHER TITLES FROM
THE ECONOMIST BOOKS

The Economist Desk Companion
The Economist Guide to Economic Indicators
The Economist Guide to the European Union
The Economist Numbers Guide
The Economist Style Guide
Going Digital
Improving Marketing Effectiveness
The International Dictionary of Finance
The Dictionary of Economics

Pocket Accounting
Pocket Director
Pocket Finance
Pocket Information Technology
Pocket Investor
Pocket Manager
Pocket Marketing
Pocket MBA
Pocket Negotiator
Pocket Strategy
Pocket Telecommunications

The Economist Pocket Asia
The Economist Pocket Europe in Figures
The Economist Pocket World in Figures

The
Economist
Books

MEASURING
BUSINESS
PERFORMANCE

Andy Neely

THE ECONOMIST IN ASSOCIATION WITH
PROFILE BOOKS LTD

Published by Profile Books Ltd
58A Hatton Garden, London ECIN 8LX

Copyright © The Economist Newspaper Ltd, 1998
Text copyright © Andy Neely 1998

All rights reserved. Without limiting the rights under copyright reserved above, no part of this publication may be reproduced, stored in or introduced into a retrieval system, or transmitted, in any form or by any means (electronic, mechanical, photocopying, recording or otherwise), without the prior written permission of both the copyright owner and the publisher of this book.

The greatest care has been taken in compiling this book.
However, no responsibility can be accepted by the publishers or compilers for the accuracy of the information presented.

Where opinion is expressed it is that of the author and does not necessarily coincide with the editorial views of The Economist Newspaper.

Typeset in EcoType by MacGuru
macguru@pavilion.co.uk

Printed in Great Britain by The Bath Press

A CIP catalogue record for this book is available
from the British Library

ISBN 1 86197 055 2

Contents

For Liese, Lizzie and Ben

Acknowledgements

IT is impossible for me to say where the ideas and concepts expressed in this book have come from. Members of the Centre for Business Performance at Cambridge University – Mohammed Al-Najjar, Mike Bourne, Jasper Hii, Mike Kennerley, Lanna Luangarpa, Dan Waggoner and Angela Walters – have undoubtedly been the source of and testbed for many of them. Other friends and colleagues, such as Mike Gregory, John Mills, Ken Platts and Huw Richards, all of the university's Institute for Manufacturing, have helped to shape my thinking about the subject more than they know over the years I have worked with them. As I reflect on the process of writing this book, three distinct phases come to mind. Between September and December 1997 I spent a wonderful few months at the University of Padova in Italy with professors Roberto Filippini, Cipriano Forza and Andrea Vinelli. Not only did they introduce me to the delights of Italy, but they also provided me with a superb location to begin the process of writing. In early 1998 I returned to Cambridge and began writing in earnest. Without the support of Liese, my wife, Lizzie and Ben, my children, and Vida Docherty, who took my scribbled notes and converted them into typed text, I doubt that I would ever have surfaced from this phase. Then, in late May, came a delightful Sunday afternoon when I was finally able to wrap up the book and send it to friends and colleagues who had kindly agreed to review the draft manuscript. Bob Kaplan and Bill Bruns of Harvard Business School, Richard Barker and Nick Oliver of the Judge Institute of Management Studies at Cambridge, Bruce Clark of Northeastern University, Bob Johnston of Warwick Business School, Marshall Meyer of the Wharton School, Tim Hewston Le Roux of 3M and Graham Lewis of Sanford UK all provided valuable and insightful comments, which undoubtedly helped me strengthen the book during the final editing process. Throughout the entire period, always there when I needed him but never interfering when I did not, was my editor, Stephen Brough. My sincere thanks and gratitude to him, to all of the others mentioned above, and to all of the authors and managers whose views and experiences I have so unashamedly borrowed and I hope built on in this book.

Andy Neely
Cambridge, October 1998

Introduction

BUSINESS performance measurement is on the agenda. New reports and articles on the topic have been appearing at a rate of one every five hours of every working day since 1994. A search of the World Wide Web reveals over 170,000 references. In 1996 one new book on the subject appeared every two weeks in the United States alone. Between 1994 and 1997 a conference company based in the UK organised 23 separate events on business performance measurement (BPM), which were attended by some 2,500 delegates from over 800 different companies, who paid over $4m for the privilege. Add to this the revenue received by other conference organisers, publishers, market research firms, software vendors and consultants and it is clear that business performance measurement is a multimillion-dollar industry.

This book asks some simple questions. The first is why? Why are so many people so interested in business performance measurement today? The main theme of the book is that the traditional view of measurement as a means of control is naive. As soon as performance measures are used as a means of control, the people being measured begin to manage the measures rather than performance. Incidents are reported selectively. Data are manipulated and presented in ways that make them look favourable. Individuals seek to undermine the measurement system. In extreme cases false data are provided and business decisions are taken on the basis of whether they will make the numbers look good, rather than whether they are good for the business. When individual and group incentives are tied to performance figures, the pressure on employees to behave in this way is even stronger. If people are rewarded for returning good figures, it is no wonder that they are motivated to take decisions and pursue courses of action that will make the figures look good, even if this means jeopardising the performance of the business as a whole.

In response to concerns such as these numerous performance measurement frameworks and alternative methods of measurement, such as the balanced scorecard[1] and shareholder value analysis[2], have been proposed. The developers of these performance frameworks and methods of measurement have, in effect, sought better ways of ensuring that the behaviours encouraged by the measures used in an organisation are consistent with that organisation's overall strategic aims. Although these approaches are valid, one of their principle weaknesses is that they ignore the most fundamental question of all: why do managers want to measure performance in the first place?

At a superficial level the answer to this question is straightforward. Managers measure because they want to know how well their organisation is performing, as this helps them to decide what they should do next. Hence the often cited homily: "You can't manage what you can't measure." Implicitly, this suggests that the primary role of measurement is to help managers understand where their organisation is now and how its performance can be improved. But this view is too simplistic. Although measurement does allow managers to assess where their organisation is and how its performance might be improved, the real value of measurement comes from the action that follows it. An organisation can have the best measurement system in the world, but unless appropriate action is taken on the basis of the information provided by the system, the performance impact will be non-existent. Furthermore, there are distinct dimensions of performance that have to be measured and managed in organisations. Some of these are non-negotiable. Failure to deliver or adhere to certain standards can result in the organisation losing its licence to operate, as former US president Richard Nixon and the Republican Party discovered to their cost during the Watergate affair. For the non-negotiable performance dimensions the role of the measurement system is to ensure compliance. Ideally, the measurement system should be designed to provide an early warning, which makes obvious the fact that unless action is taken one or more of the non-negotiable performance parameters will be infringed.

Other dimensions of performance are not so fundamental. Different customers will accept different levels of service. Different shareholders will accept different levels of financial return. An improvement programme designed to reduce defect levels by 25% may still be considered a success if defect levels are reduced by 20%. When considering the negotiable dimensions of performance the primary role of the measurement system is to allow the health of the business to be checked. In this context, measurement enables managers to establish whether the planned actions are being implemented, whether performance is improving and, if so, whether the business has a long-term future.

The data provided by the measurement system also allow the assumptions underpinning an organisation's strategies and working practices to be challenged, and they allow people to explore whether their model of how the business works is valid. Reductions in lead times are assumed to result in better delivery performance, but there is no guarantee that reducing lead times will always result in better delivery performance. By monitoring both lead times and delivery performance it is possible to use the data gathered to explore whether the predicted benefits of particular action programmes and strategies are achieved. If they are not, the strategies and action programmes can be revised.

These three roles of measurement – comply, check and challenge – are significantly different from and much richer than the traditional view of measurement as a means of control. They are not based on the assumption that the behaviour of people can be controlled through measurement. They are founded on the assumptions that measurement is a tool to be used by people to enhance business performance and that there are distinct dimensions of business performance, which need to be measured and managed in different ways. Given this starting point, one of the critical questions is: how can measurement systems for comply, check and challenge be designed, implemented and used?

The primary aims of this book are to address such questions, and in doing so to enrich the way that people think about measurement systems. The most fundamental message, especially for those responsible for the design, implementation and use of such systems, is therefore to consider from the outset what the role of the measurement system is. Is the aim to establish a means of ensuring compliance against non-negotiable performance parameters? To establish a means of checking health? Or to establish a means of challenging the assumptions which underpin the organisation's strategy by better understanding how the levers driving the business fit together? Or is the aim to achieve all three? As will be shown later in this book, the answers to these questions have fundamental implications for the structure of the measurement system that is subsequently introduced.

Chapter 1 reviews current trends in the field of business performance measurement, concentrating particularly on the measurement of customer satisfaction, employee satisfaction, intangible assets, supplier performance and financial performance. Chapter 2 explores the weaknesses of the measurement systems traditionally used in organisations and reviews the reasons for business performance measurement being on the agenda. Chapter 3 discusses in more detail why managers measure performance and sets out more fully the three roles of measurement already discussed – comply, check and challenge. Chapters 4, 5 and 6 explore each role of measurement, concentrating particularly on how to design, introduce and use appropriate measurement systems. Lastly, Chapter 7 reviews the previously discussed ideas and presents an audit framework developed to allow managers to assess the strengths and weaknesses of their organisation's existing comply, check and challenge measurement systems.

1 The business performance revolution

PERFORMANCE measurement is a topic which is often discussed but rarely defined. Literally, it is the process of quantifying past action, where measurement is the process of quantification and past action determines current performance. Organisations achieve their goals, that is they perform, by satisfying their customers with greater efficiency and effectiveness than their competitors. The terms efficiency and effectiveness are used precisely in this context. Effectiveness refers to the extent to which customer requirements are met, and efficiency is a measure of how economically the organisation's resources are utilised when providing a given level of customer satisfaction. This is an important distinction because it not only identifies the two fundamental dimensions of performance, but also highlights the fact that there can be internal as well as external reasons for pursuing specific courses of action.[1] Take, for example, one of the quality-related dimensions of performance: product reliability. In terms of effectiveness, achieving a higher level of product reliability might lead to greater customer satisfaction. In terms of efficiency, it might reduce the costs incurred by the business through decreased field failure and warranty claims. Hence the level of performance a business attains is a function of the efficiency and effectiveness of the actions it has undertaken, and thus performance measurement can be defined as the process of quantifying the efficiency and effectiveness of past action. Once this definition has been established a second immediately follows, for a performance measure can now be defined as a metric used to quantify the efficiency and/or effectiveness of a past action.

Defining what a performance measurement system constitutes, however, is not as straightforward. At one level it is simply a set of metrics used to quantify the efficiency and effectiveness of past actions. But this definition ignores the fact that a performance measurement system encompasses a supporting infrastructure. Data have to be acquired, collated, sorted, analysed, interpreted and disseminated. If any of these data-processing activities do not occur then the measurement process is incomplete and informed decisions and actions cannot subsequently take place. Hence a more complete definition is that a performance measurement system enables informed decisions to be made and actions to be taken because it quantifies the efficiency and effectiveness of past actions through the acquisition, collation, sorting, analysis, interpretation and dissemination of appropriate data. In this context, the information-processing activities are defined as follows.

- ◪ Data acquisition: the process of gathering raw facts.
- ◪ Data collation: the process of compiling the raw facts into a single data set.
- ◪ Data sorting: the process of assigning the individual facts in the data set to meaningful categories so that the data can be analysed.
- ◪ Data analysis: the process of searching for patterns which exist in the sorted data set.
- ◪ Data interpretation: the process of explaining the implications of any patterns which have been identified in the sorted data set.
- ◪ Data dissemination: the process of communicating the implications of any patterns which have been identified in the sorted data set.

These definitions are important because language in the field of performance measurement is confused. Different commentators use different words to describe the same concepts. Some talk about performance measurements, some about performance metrics, some about critical success factors and others about key performance indicators. The phrase adopted is often context dependent and, although different phrases may be used to describe the same thing, the words companies choose to use often carry an important message. Reckitt & Colman, one of the world's largest pharmaceuticals and household products companies, for example, has decided to use the phrase "development measures" rather than performance measures, because it emphasises that the role of measurement is to help the organisation develop, rather than to allow an individual's performance to be assessed. The distinction is subtle but useful, in that the phrase "development measures" eliminates some of the perceived threat of performance measurement.

Measuring the evidence of a revolution

In 1991 Bob Eccles, a former professor of business administration at Harvard Business School, wrote a paper for the *Harvard Business Review* entitled "The Performance Measurement Manifesto".[2] In it he heralded a performance measurement revolution and predicted that "within the next five years, every company will have to redesign how it measures its business performance". Current evidence suggests that he was right.

Towers Perrin, a consulting company based in the United States, surveyed 100 of its largest customers in 1996. It found that 60% of them were using a balanced scorecard to measure business performance and that the majority of this 60% had introduced their balanced scorecards during the previous two years.[3] Following its 1996 survey, the Institute of Management Accountants reported similar results. It found that 64% of American businesses were actively experimenting with new ways of measuring, collecting and reporting non-financial data.[4] A 1996 corporate performance measurement study of 312 American organisations showed that financial measures accounted for only 27% of participants' measurement criteria; the remaining 73% covered areas such as quality, customer satisfaction, productivity, workforce and market indicators.[5] On the other side of the Atlantic, a survey was conducted by a market research agency, MORI, on behalf of the UK's Centre for Tomorrow's Company. This asked business leaders whether they believed that they would best serve the needs of their shareholders by taking into account the requirements of all stakeholders – customers, employees, suppliers and members of the local community. According to MORI, 73% of business leaders in 1996 agreed that they would. This is a remarkable finding, considering that five years earlier only 20% had thought so.[6]

Performance measurement, however, is not only topical in the private sector. Its value is recognised by governments and their agencies the world over. In a 1994 white paper on competitiveness, for example, the UK government declared: "To achieve sustainable business success in the demanding world marketplace, a company must ... use relevant performance measures."[7] In the United States the National Academy of Engineering asserted: "World-class manufacturers recognise the importance of metrics in helping to define goals and performance expectations for the organisation. They adopt or develop appropriate metrics to interpret and describe quantitatively the criteria used to measure the effectiveness of the manufacturing system and its many interrelated components."[8]

Measuring the performance of government: the case of Alberta

In 1997 the third annual report on the performance of the government of Alberta, Canada, was released. The introduction suggests that the report serves two purposes:

"First, *Measuring Up* is an accountability document. It provides a report to Albertans on achievements compared with targets set. These, combined with the financial results, provide Albertans with comprehensive information on how the government has performed. Second, Measuring Up is intended to help policymakers improve the quality of programs and services for Albertans. By measuring and tracking results, we can look at what is working well and what is not. And we can make choices about whether to revise, retain, or drop certain programs."

Measuring Up contains 23 core performance measures that relate to 18 government goals. The report consists of three main sections.

1 People: measured in terms of life expectancy at birth; health status; births to children (mothers under age 18); educational attainment; literacy and numeracy; family income distribution.
2 Prosperity: measured in terms of gross domestic product; job creation; resource wealth; skill development; adoption of new technologies; cost of government; transportation to export markets; taxation load; provincial credit rating; net debt; workplace climate.
3 Preservation: measured in terms of crime rate; serious youth crime; resource sustainability; air quality; water quality; land quality.

Unlike many government reports, *Measuring Up* explicitly identifies where performance has been strong, and where improvement is required.
"Good progress has been made in:

- **Life expectancy.** Albertans have one of the highest life expectancies in the world. Life expectancy has increased since 1991.
- **Births to children (mothers under age 18).** The rate of babies born to young women under 18 dropped by 17% in 1995 compared with 1991; however, Alberta's rate is still higher than the Canadian average.
- **Literacy and numeracy skills for young Albertans.** The percentage of grade 9 students achieving acceptable standards in both language arts and math is up in 1996. Language arts scores are up from 82% to 88%, while math scores are up from 66% to 69%.
- **Family income distribution.** The number of Alberta families with incomes less than $20,000 declined to 10.3% in 1995.
- **Taxation load.** Alberta continues to have the lowest personal income tax rate in Canada.
- **Net debt.** By the end of 1996–97, net debt, excluding pension liabilities

was down to C$3.7 billion.
- **Job creation.** 157,300 jobs were created between December 1992 and December 1996, well above the target set.
- **Days lost to disputes.** Alberta continues to have a positive labour relations environment. The number of days lost to labour disputes dropped by over 50% in 1996.
- **Crime rate.** Violent crimes in Alberta have dropped by 4.9% and property crimes are down by 4.4%.
- **Air quality.** No days of poor air quality were reported in 1996.
- **Land quality.** Land productivity has improved over the 1971–80 base.

Areas for improvement include:

- **High school completion rate.** Alberta's high school completion rate remained unchanged at 69% in 1996, below the target of 75%.
- **Math scores.** Although there were improvements in 1996, math skills are still below the target of 85% of students meeting acceptable standards.
- **Births to children.** The rate of young women having children has declined significantly, but Alberta's rate is still greater than the Canadian average.
- **Private sector funding of research and development.** Alberta's rate of funding is below the comparable Canadian rate.
- **Violent crime rate.** Alberta's property crime rate has fallen below the Canadian average, but the rate of violent crimes remains slightly above the national average.
- **Serious youth crime.** The latest information for 1995–96 is not yet available, but the 1994–95 rates were significantly above the Canadian average.
- **Oil and gas reserves.** The production of conventional oil and gas has exceeded the rate of replacement, resulting in declining reserves, although we still have vast reserves of oil sands remaining.
- **Downstream water quality.** Water quality downstream from major urban centres and other developments continues to exceed recreational use guidelines for three of the province's six major rivers."

Source: Alberta government web page (http://www.treas.gov.ab.ca).

Measuring customer satisfaction

There appears to be widespread acceptance that non-financial measures should balance financial ones. Jack Welch, chief executive of General Electric, a Baldridge Award-winning company, is frequently cited as saying: "We always said that if you had three measurements to live by they'd be employee satisfaction, customer satisfaction and cash flow. If you've got cash in the till at the end, the rest is all going to work. If you've got high customer satisfaction you are going to get market share. If you've got high employee satisfaction, you're going to get productivity. And if you've got cash you know it's all working."

Customer satisfaction questionnaires are ubiquitous. It is almost impossible to stay in a hotel and not be presented with one. Indeed, some hotels have become so obsessed with measurement that they have different customer satisfaction questionnaires in the bedroom, the health club, the bar and each of the restaurants. The measurement of customer satisfaction has become an industry in itself. Software suppliers, market research agencies, universities, telecoms operators and management consultants all offer services designed to help organisations assess the satisfaction of their customers. Apian, a software company based in Seattle, for example, has developed software to help users, including companies such as Hewlett-Packard and Procter & Gamble, design questionnaires. One product, Survey Pro™, automatically sets up the data entry screens so that no database programming is required; another, IntelliCruncher™, keeps track of which figure types and statistics are valid for which questions; and a third, NetCollect™, allows data to be collected via the Internet.

In the field of market research, generalists, such as MORI and Gallup, compete directly with customer satisfaction specialists, such as J.D. Power & Associates. Founded in 1968 and with headquarters in Los Angeles, J.D. Power & Associates is probably best known for surveys relating to the automotive industry. Each year it publishes several syndicated consumer opinion studies, which together measure customer satisfaction from vehicle purchase through five years of ownership. Specific surveys include: sales satisfaction study; initial quality study; customer satisfaction study; automotive performance, executional layout (APEAL); and vehicle dependability study. Other syndicated studies include: dealer attitude study; luxury escaped shopper study; and luxury marque image study.

Measuring customer satisfaction, however, is not solely the province of well-established firms. Along with smaller market research agencies, entrepreneurial university professors have recognised the power of customer satisfaction surveys and have established centres devoted to the topic. Northern Illinois University, for example, has a Public Opinion Laboratory, which has conducted telephone interviews on behalf of 100 different public- and private-sector organisations. The Public Research Institute at the State University of San Francisco supports a Californian business, ValueStar™, which assesses the quality of service provided by Bay area businesses through extensive customer surveys (see below).

ValueStar™

ValueStar's mission is: "To make the world a better place for consumers by identifying for them those companies that have very satisfied customers. In doing so we [ValueStar™] help make businesses better." In collaboration with the Public Research Institute of San Francisco State University, ValueStar™ rates the performance of local service businesses and professional firms, awarding those that pass a licence to use the ValueStar™ symbol in their marketing programmes for one year. The rating process consists of four steps.

Step 1: Customer satisfaction rating
A random sample of approximately 400 customers is selected from the applicant company's records for the previous 12–36 months. The company cannot choose which customers the Public Research Institute contacts.

Approximately 100 customers are asked to rate how satisfied they are with the value they received from the company being rated and if they would use the company again. The customers' identities and individual responses are kept completely confidential.

Based on the customers' answers, the company's ValueStar™ customer satisfaction rating is calculated. This is compared with an industry-specific benchmark score for the Bay area that ValueStar™ has developed through research. To pass this step of the rating process the company must exceed this benchmark score for its own industry unless the benchmark score is below 82.5, in which case the company must exceed 82.5.

Step 2: Company status check
The applicant's complaint status is checked with industry-specific and general complaint bureaus.

Step 3: Company licence validation
The applicant must have a valid licence in good standing for the major services it offers to the public.

Step 4: Company insurance cover
The applicant's insurance agents must provide ValueStarTM with written certificates of insurance showing that they have workers' compensation, liability or specialised insurance coverage where necessary.

The ValueStar™ programme was launched in July 1995 and its growth has been phenomenal. By the end of 1997 over 150,000 companies had been rated. Over a two-year period ValueStar's licensees' base more than quintupled from 198 to 995. The company's revenue increased from $60,000 (in the first quarter of fiscal year 1996) to $525,000 (in the first quarter of fiscal year 1998), with each new customer generating more than $1,400 in annual revenue for ValueStar™, at margins in excess of 80%, after their first year. Given that licensee renewal rates run at 75% and over 70% of business customers purchase additional information products from ValueStar™, the management team's ambition to build a business with gross annual revenue of more than $100m by 2003 seems attainable, especially when the size of ValueStar's target market is taken into account. "The company's research indicates that there are approximately 60 different geographic regions in North America with populations exceeding 1m that have business and consumer demographics receptive to the ValueStar program. Within these markets are more than 5m prospective service and professional businesses."

Source: ValueStar home page (http://www.valuestar.com).

A key trend in the field of customer satisfaction is the ever-increasing sophistication of measurement. In the early 1980s organisations monitored how satisfied their customers were by keeping track of the number of complaints they received. The problem with this is that only one in ten dissatisfied customers complain. The other nine simply tell ten of their friends. As businesses absorbed this message, managers began to seek more pro-active ways of monitoring customer satisfaction, through customer opinion surveys and focus groups, for example. By the early 1990s people were beginning to question whether straight customer satisfaction was sufficient. Xerox found that its completely satisfied customers were six times more likely to repeat their purchase within the next 18 months than customers who were merely satisfied. A provocatively entitled paper, "Why Satisfied Customers Defect",[9] reported research which demonstrated that this phenomenon could be observed across five different industries: automobiles; personal computers purchased by businesses; hospitals; airlines; and local telephone services. A second study found that "companies can boost profits by almost 100% by retaining just 5% more of their customers".[10]

Leading businesses today are striving to measure and manage customer loyalty rather than customer satisfaction. Data on intention to repeat purchase and willingness to recommend are increasingly being sought. Customer loyalty schemes, such as frequent flier programmes and supermarket reward cards, are being introduced. The driving force behind these efforts is the realisation that keeping existing customers is likely to be more profitable than recruiting new ones. Regular pizza customers, for example, are said to be worth more than $8,000 over the life of a ten-year franchise contract, and lifetime Cadillac owners spend more than $330,000 on vehicles.[11] Frederick Reichheld, a vice-president of consultants Bain & Co, and Earl Sasser, a professor at Harvard Business School, explored how much losing a customer cost over 100 companies from two dozen industries.[12] They found that:

- Credit card companies spend, on average, $51 dollars to recruit a customer and set up a new account. It takes them almost two years to recoup this investment.
- For auto-service companies the expected profit from a fourth-year customer is more than triple the profit that same customer generates in the first year.
- As customers become more comfortable with the product or service being offered they use it more. "For one industrial distributor, net sales per account continued to rise into the 19th year of the relationship."
- "Companies can boost profits by almost 100% by retaining just 5% more of their customers."

There is a huge difference between buying and earning customer loyalty. Truly loyal customers not only buy repeatedly from the same business, but also become advocates for the business and recommend it to others. Many of the loyalty card schemes that have been introduced, most notably by supermarkets and airlines, effectively buy loyalty rather than earn it. Gifts, such as free flights and shopping coupons, are offered to those who repeatedly purchase from the organisation. In reality, most customers simply accept the gifts offered by all the organisations concerned. Hence many supermarket shoppers belong to multiple loyalty schemes. They shop wherever it is most convenient and produce the relevant loyalty card when they reach the checkout.

Strategies for measuring customer loyalty

Tracking true customer loyalty is complex, but several approaches can be adopted.

1 Ask customers directly. Hence the inclusion in many customer satisfaction questionnaires of questions such as: "How likely are you to use this service again?" and "Would you be willing to recommend this business to a friend?"

2 Track purchasing habits, especially of those customers who are not members of loyalty schemes, because if they repeat their purchases they are not doing so because they have been bribed. Credit card data, invoice records and enquiry databases are all valuable sources of information.

3 Identify the proportion of new customers that come to the business following the recommendation of a friend. The higher the proportion, the greater is the level of loyalty within the existing customer base.

4 Deliberately flex prices. This is the most dramatic approach. Loyal customers are likely to be less price sensitive than are disloyal customers. By selectively flexing prices it is possible to establish the extent of loyalty within the customer base.

Measuring employee satisfaction

As the Jack Welch quote on page 10 suggests, there are dimensions of business performance other than customer satisfaction it is important to measure. Employee satisfaction surveys have now become common practice. Since it was established in 1974, International Survey Research (ISR) has measured and monitored employee satisfaction in over 1,800 client organisations in 92 countries, surveying more than 27m employees in the process. Research conducted in the UK suggests that 76% of *Financial Times* 500 companies survey their employees on an annual or biennial basis.[13] The fundamental question is: does employee satisfaction matter? Most people assume that satisfied employees are more productive and hence perform better, but is this true? Numerous researchers have sought to answer this question, and the consensus in the academic community is that a weak but positive correlation exists between employee satisfaction and employee performance. On a more positive note, a 1997 study by researchers from the Institute of Work Psychology at the University of Sheffield found a strong correlation between employee satisfaction, employee organisational commitment and overall business performance.

- 12% of the variation in profitability among companies can be explained by variations in job satisfaction of their employees. Moreover, 13% of the variation in profitability among companies can be explained by the differences in employee organisational commitment.
- 25% of the variation in subsequent productivity of companies can be explained by job satisfaction of employees, even controlling for size and unionisation. In comparison, 17% of the variation in company productivity is explained by employee organisational commitment.
- When both employee organisational commitment and job satisfaction are examined together, job satisfaction emerges as the most significant predictor of variation in companies' subsequent performance.[14]

Research completed in 1998 by Gallup in the United States suggests even more dramatic results. Gallup reports that organisations achieving higher levels of employee satisfaction than their rivals outperform them by 22% in terms of productivity, 38% in terms of customer satisfaction, 27% in terms of profitability and 22% in terms of employee retention.[15]

Measuring intellectual capital

Closely aligned with employee satisfaction is the notion of human or intellectual capital, a topic which is growing in importance as businesses seek to compete on the basis of their intellectual as well as their technical assets. People are only just beginning to understand how these assets can be nurtured, protected and valued. Gordon Petrash, global director of intellectual asset and capital management at Dow Chemical Company, reports that Dow, "like most organisations ... had a firm grasp on the indicators that monitored how well hard assets produced value, but lacked even a basic language for talking about intellectual assets in terms of how they were brought together and valued".[16] To demonstrate the importance of developing such a language, Petrash and his team decided to start by analysing Dow's patent portfolio. They adopted a six-step process, which involved:

- **Strategy setting:** balancing investment between the intellectual activities required to develop new technology and those needed to maintain current business or improve competitiveness.
- **Competitor analysis:** assessment of the strategies, intangible assets and capabilities of key competitors.
- **Classification:** reviewing and classifying the current in-house asset portfolio; defining what intangible assets are owned, what they are used for and where ownership is assigned.
- **Valuation:** placing a value on the current in-house assets. Making an inventory of their acquisition and maintenance costs, and determining the actions needed to maximise their value within the business strategy. This may involve maintaining the asset, licensing it out or abandoning it.
- **Future assets required:** defining which knowledge assets will be required in future years and deciding whether to develop these in-house or acquire them from outside sources.
- **Document the portfolio:** assemble the portfolio of new knowledge and repeat the entire process regularly.[17]

In the early 1990s Dow, which spends $1 billion per year on research and development, held over 29,000 patents. As a direct result of the process outlined above, 200 of these were classified as core and 4,350 were labelled "vanity patents", taken out because engineers wanted their names on patents, not because they were of any real value to the business. As Gordon McConnachie, Dow's intellectual asset manager, points out, the associated cost savings were significant: "Full analysis of the 29,000 patents in the Dow corporate portfolio has reduced the patent tax maintenance costs due by $40m over its ten-year life. Annual patent acquisition costs are $1m lower due to better alignment of activity with business strategy. Policy is now to increase licensing revenue to $125m in 1995 through the licensing out of elements of Dow's core technologies."[18] The cost savings, however, are not the most important part of the equation. Dow has now identified the fundamental technical and

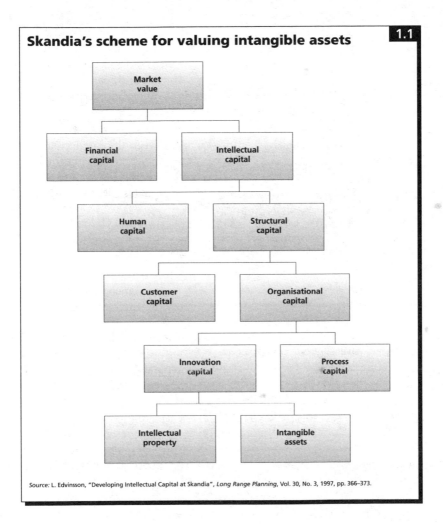

1.1
Skandia's scheme for valuing intangible assets

Source: L. Edvinsson, "Developing Intellectual Capital at Skandia", *Long Range Planning*, Vol. 30, No. 3, 1997, pp. 366–373.

intellectual building blocks of its future. Instead of dissipating resources and attention equally across 29,000 different patents, it can focus on 200 and let the others wither, or milk them through licence fees.

There is more to intellectual capital than simply managing patents. Leif Edvinsson, vice-president of intellectual capital at Skandia, a Swedish insurance company, suggests that intellectual capital can best be managed by breaking down the market value of a company into its constituent elements: financial capital and intellectual capital (see Figure 1.1). According to Edvinsson, intellectual capital further subdivides into

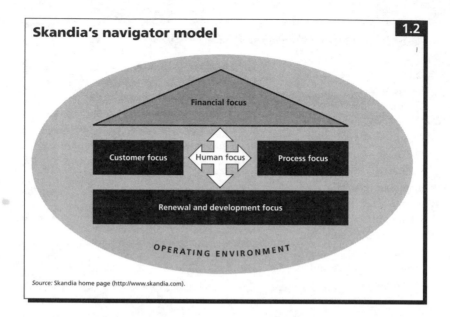

Skandia's navigator model `1.2`

Financial focus

Customer focus Human focus Process focus

Renewal and development focus

OPERATING ENVIRONMENT

Source: Skandia home page (http://www.skandia.com).

human capital and structural capital, with the latter consisting of customer capital and organisational capital. "Within organisational capital the value of processes could be extracted leaving innovation capital as the balancing value. Within the innovation capital it is possible to identify the value of intellectual properties such as patents, trade marks, and so on. This leaves intangible assets as the balancing value."[19]

Since 1995 Skandia has been attempting to value its intangible assets. To publicise its work the company has been releasing supplements to its annual report. The first report, "Visualising Intellectual Capital", was published in May 1995 as a supplement to the 1994 annual report. The most recent, "Customer Capital", is available on the World Wide Web and describes both Skandia's approach to the management of intellectual capital and how the business has sought to value it. At the heart of Skandia's intellectual capital valuation methodology is a balanced measurement framework known as the Skandia Navigator, which consists of five building blocks: financial focus; customer focus; human focus; process focus; and renewal and development focus (see Figure 1.2). Typical measures under each of these dimensions include:

- ◪ Financial focus: gross premiums written per employee; value added per employee; personal expenses; total company expenses;

Table 1.1 **SkandiaLink's Navigator model**

	1993	1994	1995	1996
Financial focus				
Gross premiums written (MSEK)	1,145	1,874	2,087	2,413
Operating result (MSEK)	137	132	176	179
Assets under management (MSEK)	2,273	3,670	5,699	9,202
Customer focus				
Number of contracts	74,300	115,000	153,100	182,900
Surrender rate (%)	n/a	1.0	1.5	1.7
Human focus				
Number of employees	52	51	48	45
Human capital index				
(maximum value = 1,000)	n/a	534	493	426
Employees with secondary education				
or higher (%)	n/a	74	73	3
Employees with 3 or more years' service (%)	n/a	62	88	92
Process focus				
Administrative expense/gross				
premiums written (%)	5.7	4.5	5.0	4.1
IT expense/administrative expense (%)	26.0	28.0	27.1	26.3
Renewal and development focus				
Number of contracts/employee	1,439	2,253	3,180	4,064
Fund switches via Telelink (%)	n/a	22	40	50

Source: Skandia home page (http://www.skandia/com).

education investment against gross written premiums.
- ◪ Customer focus: telephone accessibility; accounts per employee; satisfied customer index; number of depositors.
- ◪ Human focus: average age; average length of service; numbers of people in leadership positions; level of empowerment.
- ◪ Process focus: IT literate employees; payroll costs versus administration expenses; net operating income per square metre; cost per square metre.
- ◪ Renewal and development focus: education investments per employee; numbers with degrees; growth in gross premiums written; percentage increase in assets under Skandia's management.

Each of Skandia's six business units, which together serve over 8m customers, values its own intellectual capital through its own customised Navigator model. SkandiaLink, the leading unit-linked assurance company in the Swedish life market, for example, monitors the performance parameters shown in Table 1.1 on the previous page. According to Edvinsson, the process of producing these reports, and hence explicitly discussing Skandia's Intellectual Capital, has several benefits: "The Navigator model provides balanced reporting by adding ratios for intellectual capital to traditional financial measures. This process leads us to a whole, systematic management of hidden value, which also helps us cultivate investor and customer relationships. That is why we publish the Intellectual Capital supplement to our annual report."

Skandia has now begun experimenting with "futures centres". These provide an environment where individuals can speculate about the future of Skandia and the markets in which it operates without fear of sanction or censure. One of the advantages of these centres is that they legitimise the process of questioning the values and norms which underlie Skandia's strategy and business practices, an essential activity given that Skandia wishes its members to challenge continuously the organisation's strategy.

Strategies for tracking intellectual capital

Intellectual capital, by its nature, is inherently difficult to quantify, but as the information society gathers pace and the knowledge economy emerges, intellectual capital will become an ever greater proportion of an organisation's assets and hence ever more important to quantify and manage. The simplest way of estimating an organisation's intellectual capital is to examine the difference between its enterprise value and its book value. The enterprise value is calculated by estimating the net present value of the organisation's future cash flows. This is equivalent to establishing, in today's money, the total value of all the future net cash flows the organisation will generate. The book value is calculated by reviewing the value of all the organisation's tangible assets, such as land, machinery, factories and raw materials. Depending upon the country in which the organisation is operating, the book value will also include some intangible assets, such as patents, brands and development expenses in the UK and purchased goodwill in the United States. (Purchased goodwill is the goodwill a firm captures following its acquisition of another firm. When one firm acquires another it purchases not only the latter's tangible assets, but also its intangible assets, including any goodwill. In the United States this purchased goodwill is formally valued in the balance sheet following the acquisition, and then subsequently written off, typically over a period of 20 years.)

Although this approach sounds straightforward, there are some problems. The first is that it is only possible to estimate the enterprise value. The second is that sometimes the book value can be greater than the enterprise value, which implicitly places a negative value on the organisation's intellectual capital. In reality this is impossible. An organisation can possess no intellectual capital, or at least its intellectual capital can be of no value, but it cannot possess negative intellectual capital. Hence the best way of valuing intellectual capital is to accept that the value of any organisation's intellectual capital must be zero or greater, depending on that organisation's enterprise value.

Measuring supplier performance

So far two ingredients core to all businesses have been discussed, namely customers and employees. For many organisations there is a third: suppliers. Once again there is evidence of considerable activity in the evaluation of supplier performance. Since the mid-1980s, for example, most of the major players in the automotive industry have been subjecting their suppliers to formal assessment and accreditation programmes. There have been two reasons for this. First, car assemblers have been seeking to drive improvements in supplier performance and reduce costs in the supplier-customer relationship. Second, they have used these programmes to help them decide which suppliers to dispense with and which to build partnerships with, as they have rationalised their supply bases.

Supplier assessment at Rover

The Rover Group, a subsidiary of BMW, introduced a new supplier performance report in early 1998. This is sent quarterly to all Rover suppliers and summarises Rover Group's perception of supplier performance across the following dimensions: quality; cost; delivery;

partnership; and overall. The report consists of two sections. The first summarises the supplier's overall performance and highlights any areas of concern. The second breaks down each of the top level measures into their constituent elements. Quality, for example, is measured in terms of:

- delivered quality (parts per million);
- delivered quality (incidents);
- warranty claims (category 1, parts per million);
- critical actions;
- quality problem resolution;
- quality and environmental systems.

To calculate the supplier's overall quality performance, each of the above dimensions is weighted and scored (see Figure 1.3).

Similar accreditation schemes operate at a more global level. ISO 9000, for example, is the internationally recognised quality standard. There are numerous examples of organisations declaring that they will not buy from suppliers who have not achieved ISO 9000 certification. The Spanish rail operator, RENFE, has introduced a substantial supplier accreditation programme. This consists of four phases: registration; assessment; approval; accreditation. In the registration phase potential suppliers are invited simply to register their interest in being a supplier to RENFE. In the assessment phases all suppliers are asked to complete a self-assessment questionnaire based on the European Foundation for Quality Management (EFQM) model. This consists of 110 questions covering the following topics: leadership; personnel management; policy and strategy; resources; processes; staff satisfaction; customer satisfaction; social impact; and company results. Performance is scored on a five-point scale, with five being the highest score.

Once potential suppliers have completed their self-assessments and submitted the information, RENFE sends in its own assessors. The differences in scores can be startling (see Table 1.2 on page 24), but they are valuable because they highlight areas where there are mismatches in perception, caused by any one of the following:

- The supplier thinking it is better (or worse) than it actually is.
- RENFE not understanding how good (or bad) the supplier actually is.

Rover Group's supplier performance report: example calculation

1.3

PROCESS STEPS

Step 1 – Compare actual performance with the performance benchmarks (column A) to determine performance scores (column B).

Step 2 – Identify if any demerits have been incurred (column C).

Step 3 – Identify the weighting factor for each measure (columns D and E).

Step 4 – Calculate the actual score (column F) for each measure (column B x column E).

Step 5 – Calculate the maximum score (column G) for each measure (3 x column E); a score of 3 represents class-leading performance against each measure.

Step 6 – Calculate the sum of the actual scores and the sum of the maximum scores (subtotals).

Step 7 – Divide the total actual score by the total maximum score.

Step 8 – Convert the value to a percentage and take away all demerits to determine the section score (eg. quality, cost).

Step 9 – Calculate the sum of the section scores and divide by the number of sections to calculate the overall RG2000 supplier performance score.

QUALITY PERFORMANCE	A Actual performance	B Score awarded	C Demerit applied	D Weighting	E Weighting factor	F Actual score	G Maximum score	H Demerits	I Comments
Q1 Delivered quality (PPM)	1,068	1	n/a	Critical	x3	3	9	n/a	PPM Category C
Q2 Delivered quality (incidents)	84	0	n/a	Significant	x1	0	3	n/a	
Q3 Warranty (Cat 1 – PPM)	4	3	n/a	Critical	x3	9	9	n/a	
Q4 Critical action	A	n/a	0%	n/a	n/a	n/a	n/a	0%	
Q5 Problem resolution (quality)	C	n/a	25%	n/a	n/a	n/a	n/a	25%	
Q6 Management systems certification	ISO9001	2	n/a	Significant	x1	2	3	n/a	
Subtotals						14	24	25%	

CALCULATION

Quality rating = [(weighted score/maximum score) x 100%] – [all demerits]

$$= [(14/24) \times 100] - [25]$$
$$= [58.3] - [25]$$
$$= 33\%$$

Source: Example of scoring system distributed by Rover Group to its suppliers.

Table 1.2 **Differences in perception between RENFE and suppliers**

Scores	Self-assessment (%)	RENFE's assessment (%)
1–2	2	23
2–3	31	45
3–4	50	30
4–5	17	2

Source: Fernando Temino, director of quality implementation for RENFE, speaking at a Business Intelligence conference on business performance measurement in February 1997.

- The supplier underestimating RENFE's expectations, and hence thinking that its performance is acceptable when it is not.
- The supplier overestimating RENFE's performance expectations, and hence striving to achieve too high a level of performance, therefore introducing unnecessary cost.

Sometimes RENFE's and the supplier's assessments are consistent, but even then the information is valuable. If both parties agree that performance is unacceptable an opportunity for improvement has been identified. If both parties agree that performance is acceptable the question becomes: how can this level of performance be maintained, exploited and the reasons for it communicated to others in RENFE's supply network?

Once agreement on the scores has been reached, RENFE asks the suppliers to provide documentary evidence for every item scored 4 or 5, and improvement plans for every item scored 1 or 2. Often RENFE will help suppliers draw up their improvement plans, so that they can benefit from RENFE's experience and knowledge of how other suppliers have solved particular problems.

Supplier approval is granted only when all the improvement plans have been submitted and reviewed, but even then suppliers are not accredited. Before RENFE awards them any contracts suppliers also have to attain ISO 9000 certification. By early 1997 RENFE had taken 135 suppliers, together accounting for $250m of business, through this process. Two-thirds of the remaining 600 suppliers ($1,000m of business) had presented quality improvement programmes.

As with customer satisfaction, the measures used to track supplier performance have become increasingly sophisticated over the years.

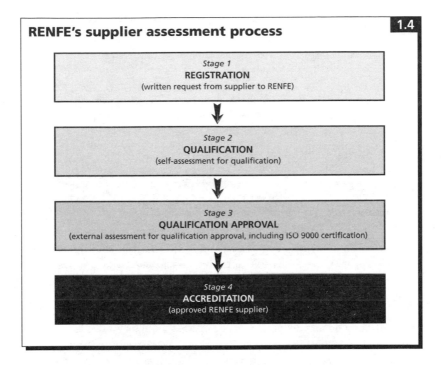

RENFE's supplier assessment process `1.4`

Stage 1
REGISTRATION
(written request from supplier to RENFE)

Stage 2
QUALIFICATION
(self-assessment for qualification)

Stage 3
QUALIFICATION APPROVAL
(external assessment for qualification approval, including ISO 9000 certification)

Stage 4
ACCREDITATION
(approved RENFE supplier)

Initially, purchasers concentrated primarily on price. Customer-supplier partnerships were almost non-existent. Instead, the role of the procurement function was to negotiate hard and acquire goods and services at the cheapest possible cost. By the early 1990s, however, more and more people were talking about the benefits of managing supply chains. Partnership became fashionable. Instead of concentrating on purchase price alone, organisations began to take a more rounded view of supplier performance. Supplier appraisal schemes covering quality, dependability, speed and flexibility became more common. Some organisations began to introduce measures such as total acquisition cost, recognising that the product cost is only a fraction of the total cost of procurement. Today the most advanced organisations ask their suppliers to comment on their performance as customers, because they recognise that turbulence in the supply chain leads to inefficiencies and hence increased cost. They ask their suppliers to help them understand what actions they can take to eliminate turbulence. Typically, this involves asking questions such as:

◪ How often do we place unacceptable demands on you?
◪ How often do we change schedules?
◪ How often are we late in making payment to you?

The message this sends to the suppliers is that the customer organisations really do want to work in partnership with them. The answers received enable the customer organisations to identify how they disrupt the supply chain, thereby highlighting which of their processes have to be enhanced.

Strategies for tracking supplier performance

When developing methods of tracking supplier performance it is crucial to recognise that not all suppliers are equally important. Commodity goods, for example, are widely available and often at comparatively low cost because there are many different sources of supply. For such goods it is rarely worth developing a close relationship with a particular supplier. It is still important to track supplier performance, but if the supplier fails to meet the demand an alternative source of supply can be easily found. The goods provided by other suppliers, however, can be critical to the organisation. Sometimes because they are product critical, that is, of strategic importance to the functionality of the product being manufactured. Sometimes because they are process critical, that is, of strategic importance to the processing of the product, perhaps because they are fitted during a bottleneck operation and hence if they are unavailable the whole operation has to stop. The last category covers goods that are not product critical, process critical, or commodity. Instead they are leveraged. Either the purchaser or the supplier will hold negotiating advantage, possibly because of the relative size of the two organisations involved. In such cases alternative sources of supply may be available, but they are unlikely to be readily available. Hence, as far as the customer is concerned, there is a greater need for partnership when purchasing leveraged goods than when purchasing commodity goods, although the need is not as great as when the goods are either product or process critical.

In developing a strategy for tracking supplier performance the first question to be asked is: which of these four categories – commodity, leveraged, product critical, process critical – do the goods being supplied fall into? Only when it has been answered can the appropriate performance measures be identified. For commodity goods the most

Measures for tracking supplier performance 1.5

CATEGORY OF GOODS BEING SUPPLIED	APPROPRIATE MEASUREMENT STRATEGY
Product/process critical	Quality of relationship (how good are we as a customer)
Leveraged goods	Supplier assessment: quality, dependability, speed and flexibility
Commodity goods	Total acquisition cost

INCREASING DEPENDENCE

appropriate measure will be total acquisition cost, that is, purchase price plus associated costs (stock holding, inspection, carriage and administration). Suppliers of commodity goods, who are able to guarantee quality and deliver direct to the line, for example, eliminate the need to hold stock and inspect. Hence they may be offering a better deal than another supplier, who can deliver only in large batches, even if the cost of the second supplier's goods is slightly lower. For product or process critical goods, however, total acquisition cost will be only one of several measures adopted. Others, which relate to quality, dependability, speed, flexibility and the quality of the customer-supplier relationship will also be necessary (see Figure 1.5).

Measuring financial performance

Much of the discussion so far has focused on the non-financial dimensions of business performance. But what about the financial dimensions? What evidence is there of a revolution there? In recent years several innovative methods of product costing and business valuation have been introduced, including activity-based costing, shareholder value analysis, economic value analysis, market value analysis and throughput

Table 1.3 **The world's most valuable brands**

Brand	Brand value in 1997 ($ bn)
Coca-Cola	47.99
Marlboro	47.64
IBM	23.70
McDonald's	19.94
Disney	17.07
Sony	14.46
Kodak	14.44
Intel	13.27
Gillette	11.99
Budweiser	11.99
Nike	11.13
Kellogg's	10.67
AT&T	10.39
Nescafé	10.34
GE	10.29
Hewlett-Packard	9.42
Pepsi	9.32
Microsoft	8.99
Frito-Lay	8.99
Levi's	8.17

Source: William, J., "Shimmering Symbols of the Modern Age", Financial Times, October 17th 1997.

accounting. One of the most topical areas is the valuation of intangible assets. The importance of this becomes apparent when considering the difference between the book value and market capitalisation of some of the world's largest companies. Take, for example, Coca-Cola. In 1995 the Coca-Cola brand, which was then 110 years old, was said to have grown by 6%. That year the company estimated its worth at $39 billion, which is equivalent to about 42% of the company's entire market value. Yet, in accounting terms, it is worth almost nothing.[20] Institutional investors and analysts recognise the value of such assets (see Table 1.3). They recognise the need for businesses to protect and nurture them. Increasingly they are demanding evidence not only of the value of the brand, but also that the necessary investments to protect the brand future are being made (see "The case for value reporting" opposite").

The case for value reporting

Research conducted by MORI on behalf of PricewaterhouseCoopers, identifies a significant gap between the information analysts would like to see companies release and the information that they actually release. MORI interviewed 107 UK analysts, asking in which of the following areas companies were seriously deficient in terms of the information they released.

Area	% of respondents
R&D productivity	47
Intellectual property	32
New product development	26
R&D investment amounts	21

Source: Coleman, I., and Eccles, R., *Pursuing Value: Reporting Gaps in the United Kingdom*, PricewaterhouseCoopers, 1997.

These findings are important because they underlie the fact that, despite conventional wisdom, the financial community recognises the value of non-financial measures. As part of its Inquiry into the Role of Tomorrow's Company the Royal Society of Arts (RSA) asked a series of senior executives what information they thought the institutional investors required: "The perception within companies is that their discussions with investors lead them to neglect long-term strategies in the interests of immediate financial returns. Investors are perceived as placing a relatively low priority on the business fundamentals – such as customer loyalty, investment in people and supplier relationship – which will determine long-term success".[21]

It then asked representatives of the investment community what information they would like and found: "The perception within the investment community is that companies are preoccupied with immediate returns and are reluctant to volunteer information about the fundamentals."[22]

The RSA describes this situation as the "dialogue of the deaf", because neither group really understands the other's interests and needs. However, there has been some evidence to suggest that this is changing.

Derek Wanless, chief executive of NatWest, one of the UK's largest high street banks, is reported to have said: "One of the weaknesses of the banking industry is that our traditional performance measures have always been biased towards external financial reporting. They have not measured the broader values in terms of quality, service and speed. Financial measures have not lead us to innovate and learn to motivate longer-term behaviours."

Further research on value reporting, conducted by Pricewaterhouse-Coopers in both the UK and the United States, suggests that both analysts and investors are frustrated by the lack of information disclosed in company accounts, although analysts are reported to be more frustrated than investors.[23] Similar research conducted by the Ernst & Young Centre for Business Innovation found that non-financial criteria contribute on average 35% to the investor's decision about which stock to purchase in the United States.[24]

In response, some organisations have begun releasing alternative annual reports, and others have adopted the strategy of issuing addenda to their existing reports. The message is clear. Performance measurement is on the agenda of investors and analysts, as well as managers, consultants and academics. Bob Eccles's revolution certainly seems to be upon us. The question this raises is why? This is what the next chapter seeks to address.

2 Reasons for revolution

R EVOLUTIONS are usually caused by unrest. The business performance revolution is no exception. So what is the basis of unrest in the context of business performance measurement? Or, more succinctly, why is business performance measurement on the agenda? This chapter argues that there are two primary reasons. First, the performance measurement systems traditionally used by organisations are fundamentally flawed. Second, there are some clear business drivers which have not only exposed these fundamental flaws, but also offered ways of overcoming them. This chapter explores both these themes in more detail by addressing two questions:

- In what ways are the measurement systems traditionally used by businesses fundamentally flawed?
- What are the drivers that have put BPM on the management agenda today?

Measure the wrong things and things will go wrong

Stories that illustrate the consequences of poorly designed performance measures abound. British Telecom (BT), for example, used to measure how long it took operators to answer phones. It stopped when it discovered that if the figures looked bad, managers would instruct operators to busy out the lines, that is, make them ring engaged.[1] A major retail bank used to measure the percentage of customer enquiries dealt with within 60 seconds. It stopped when it found that operators were cutting customers off after 59 seconds if their problems had not been solved. The senior managers of a cross-channel ferry company were delighted to find their customer service team were achieving the company targets and satisfactorily responding to all customer complaints within five working days, until they realised that they were only doing so by issuing full refunds to everyone who wrote in.

These and countless other examples illustrate that businesses have some fundamental problems with the performance measures they use. Critics of traditional performance measures point out that they are historical in focus; that they encourage short termism; and that they often result in local optimisation. Measures such as machine or labour utilisation encourage supervisors to keep machines and people busy producing products, even when there is no market demand. In extreme cases, local efficiencies can seem remarkable, but the business can be left to write off vast quantities of obsolete inventory.

Designing robust performance measures

It is easy to underestimate how hard it is to design good performance measures, and the examples above illustrate the dysfunctional behaviours that can result. To avoid this the designers of measures must consider during the design process the behaviours a measure will encourage once it has been implemented. A useful framework for doing this is provided by the performance measure record sheet (see Figure 2.1 on page 36). This encapsulates the awkward questions designers of measures need to ask themselves when deciding which measures to implement.

When designing a performance measure people generally think about two things: the title and the formula. But for the measure to be of practical value, there are many other dimensions that must be considered. These include: the frequency of measurement; the frequency of review; where the data will come from; the rationale for introducing the measure; and, perhaps most importantly, who will act on the data when they become available and what they will do.

The purpose of a measure, for example, is often not properly considered. Managers may wish to measure employee satisfaction to gauge the likelihood of staff retention. Or they may wish to use a measure of employee satisfaction to establish whether morale has improved since the last employee satisfaction survey. Different measures of employee satisfaction are required to satisfy these different purposes. In the first case a barometer of employee satisfaction, which allows managers to gauge individuals' perceptions and explore whether they believe that they would be happier working for someone else, would be appropriate. In the second case a measure which audited whether the concerns raised by employees during the previous employee satisfaction survey had been dealt with would be more effective.

Defining the formula carefully is also important because the formula affects the way people behave. A good example of this is provided by a measure such as time to quote. Some years ago the management team of an automotive components business had a number of concerns, two of which were most germane to the issue of time to quote. The first was simply that it was taking the sales teams too long to generate and submit quotations. The second was that the sales teams were not interacting sufficiently with the customers. The organisation had recently restructured and introduced a new set of sales teams that were based around particular customers. Hence it had a Ford team, a General Motors team, a Nissan team, a Toyota team, and so on. In introducing the teams it had been necessary to gather together different groups of people – sales managers, engineers and designers. Because the teams were new the team members were spending time getting to know each other and this reduced the amount of time they had for customers. Hence the business had two problems: one was how to reduce the length of time it took to produce quotations; the other was how to increase the amount of contact with customers.

Measuring time to quote is like any measure of lead time. In defining the formula it is necessary to specify when to start the clock ticking and when to stop it. The natural response is to start the clock ticking when the customer first contacts the organisation. But customers often do not provide all the information necessary to produce a quote when they first make contact. They might give an incomplete specification, incomplete time scales or incomplete material requirements, so the sales team usually cannot start the process of producing quotations. One of the fundamental tenets of performance measurement is that it is not fair to measure people on something over which they have no control. Hence starting the clock ticking at the point when the customer first makes contact seems unreasonable. The problem, however, is that if you do not this legitimises the sales staff not working on certain quotations, even if these contain a new piece of work from a strategically important customer. The alternative is to define the start point for the quotation process as the point at which the customer first makes contact. The advantage is that this encourages positive behaviour. It encourages sales people to develop a proforma or a checklist that they use to capture information when customers telephone to ask for a quotation. For example, the checklist might ask the sales people to make sure they collect information about what materials the customer wants, when the design specification will be available, and so on. Such a form is simple but it begins to put the onus for managing the quote generation process back into the hands of the sales person, which is where it needs to be.

Remember that this business had two problems. The first was reducing time to quote; the second was encouraging the sales team to talk to the customers more. It overcame the second problem by subtle design of the formula for the measure, in terms of when to stop the clock. The natural response is to say that the clock should stop when the quotation goes in the envelope or in the fax machine to the customer. The managers of this business decided that they would not allow the process to be signed off, that is, the clock to be stopped, until verbal confirmation of receipt of the quotation had been received from the customer. The behaviour this formula encourages is for sales people to phone the customer after they have faxed the quotation and check whether it has been received. While on the phone the sales person may as well ask the customer if the quotation was comprehensive, if there was anything else that was needed or if the order was likely to be granted. Hence by careful design of the formula it is possible to encourage desirable behaviours in the organisation.

Other organisations have used other ways of encouraging people to respond to particular performance measures. An aerospace company reviewed the way in which it collected information on emerging technologies. It realised that it had a purchasing organisation with some 800 people in it. The majority of these people were talking to and visiting suppliers on a regular basis. It occurred to the management team that if they could introduce a process of capturing information on emerging technologies through their routine visits and discussions with suppliers, they would be in a powerful position. They therefore introduced a new proforma, which required people to report on technologies observed during visits to suppliers. To assess how well the embedding of this new process was working, the management team also introduced a new performance measure, namely number of completed technology assessment forms. To ensure that people realised that the management team were serious about this, they photocopied technology assessment forms on to the back of the expense claim form. Anyone submitting an expense claim for a visit was told that unless they completed the technology assessment form their expense claim would not be processed. Hence through careful design of the way in which the data for this measure were collected, the management team were able to emphasise how much they cared about the measure and, much more importantly, the process of capturing the relevant information on emerging technologies.

Awkward questions to ask when completing the performance measure record sheet

Box 1 Measure
- What should the measure be called?
- Does the title explain what the measure is?
- Does it explain why the measure is important?
- Is it a title that everyone will understand?

Box 2 Purpose
- Why is the measure being introduced?
- What is the aim of the measure?
- What behaviours should the measure encourage?

Box 3 Target
- What level of performance is desirable?
- How long will it take to reach this level of performance?
- How does this level of performance compare with the competition?
- How good is the competition currently?
- How fast is the competition improving?

Box 4 Formula
- How can this dimension of performance be measured?
- Can the formula be defined in mathematical terms?
- Is the formula clear?
- Does the formula explain exactly what data are required?
- What behaviour will the formula induce?
- Are there any other behaviours that the formula should induce?
- Is the scale being used appropriate?
- How accurate will the data generated be?
- Are the data accurate enough?
- If an average is used how much data will be lost?
- Is the loss of data acceptable?
- Would it be better to measure the spread of performance?

Box 5 Frequency
- How often should this measure be made?
- How often should this measure be reported?

Performance measure record sheet `2.1`

Measure	
Purpose	
Target	
Formula	
Frequency	
Who measures?	
Source of data	
Who acts on the data?	
What do they do?	
Notes	

Box 6 Who measures?
- ◪ Who, by name, is actually responsible for making this measure?

Box 7 Source of data
- ◪ Where will the data to make this measure come from?

Box 8 Who acts on the data?
- ◪ Who, by name, is actually responsible for ensuring that performance along this dimension improves?

Box 9 What do they do?
- ◪ What actions will they take to ensure that performance along this dimensions improves?

Measuring history

Most traditional measures are historically oriented. Imagine driving a car using only a rearview mirror to steer by. Picture trying to play a game of tennis by watching the scoreboard, rather than the ball and your opponent. It would be hopeless. Yet many traditional measures are like rearview mirrors or tennis scoreboards. They tell you what happened last week, last month or last year, but provide no indication of what might be about to happen next. As Graham Ward, deputy chairman of World Energy Group at PricewaterhouseCoopers, points out, predictions about future performance are really what matter: "It is a sad fact that accounting has often been criticised for reporting today about what has happened the day before yesterday, when what people are really interested in hearing about is tomorrow."[2]

An illustration of the fallacy of measuring history is provided by a measure such as sales turnover. This is undoubtedly a valuable measure – no one would want shares in a business that did not track its sales turnover – but it is important to consider how the measure can be used on an operational basis. The following extract of a discussion with the sales director of a major automotive components company illustrates a common failing of businesses to measure the right things.

Q   Why do you measure sales turnover?
SD   Because it tells me how well sales are holding up.
Q   Why do you need to know how well sales are holding up?
SD   Because part of my job is to ensure that we meet our sales targets.
Q   Why does a measure of sales turnover help you ensure that you meet your sales targets?
SD   Well … it doesn't exactly help me ensure that we meet our sales targets, but it does help me tell whether we met last month's targets.
Q   Why do you need to know whether you met last month's targets?
SD   Because … one of the things we discuss at the board meeting is whether we met last month's sales targets. So it is important for me to know in advance the level of performance we achieved and the reasons for any performance shortfall.
Q   Why don't you discuss next month's anticipated performance at the board meeting? Would a measure of orders received, or quotes submitted not be better for managing sales turnover?

Identifying predictive, leading or forward-looking measures, such as the value of quotes submitted or the book to bill ratio (the number of orders received compared with the numbers of orders invoiced in a given

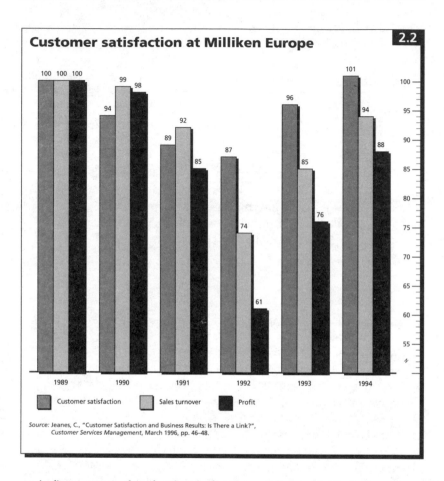

Customer satisfaction at Milliken Europe 2.2

Customer satisfaction   Sales turnover   Profit

Source: Jeanes, C., "Customer Satisfaction and Business Results: Is There a Link?",
Customer Services Management, March 1996, pp. 46–48.

period), as opposed to lagging indicators, such as sales turnover, is not easy, although several organisations have made some progress. Milliken Europe, for example, has been able to identify a correlation between customer satisfaction and financial performance, with an 18–24 month time lag (see Figure 2.2).

British Telecom has used the data it collects through customer satisfaction surveys in a similar way. Following extensive analysis it has been able to establish that a key driver of customer satisfaction is quality of service, which in turn is driven by the account management, sales, repair, provision and inquiry processes (see Figure 2.3).

Art Schneiderman, former director of quality and productivity improvement at Analogue Devices, has developed a measure known as

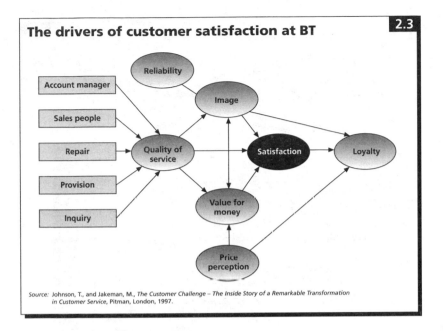

The drivers of customer satisfaction at BT

2.3

Source: Johnson, T., and Jakeman, M., *The Customer Challenge – The Inside Story of a Remarkable Transformation in Customer Service*, Pitman, London, 1997.

the improvement half-life.[3] He has demonstrated that the time taken to improve performance by 50% remains constant. That is, if it takes six months to reduce defect levels by 50%, from 100 parts per million to 50 parts per million, then it should take a further six months to reduce defect levels to 25 parts per million, assuming the amount of resource and the level of attention devoted to the problem remain constant (see Figure 2.4 on the next page).

The strength of all of these measurement systems lies in their predictive capability. Applying them enables management to manage future business performance better. As Clive Jeanes of Milliken says: "The survey data provided a wonderful early warning indicator of potential problems ... if corrective action were taken quickly, in response to the warning signals, the problem could be averted. But if the business management chose to ignore the warning signs, retribution would follow in the form of worsening financial results and other performance indicators."[4]

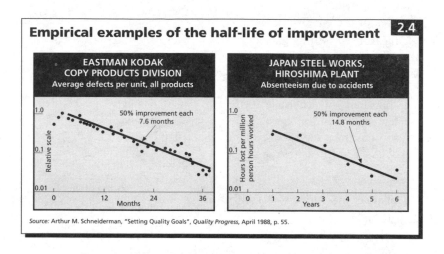

Empirical examples of the half-life of improvement · 2.4

Source: Arthur M. Schneiderman, "Setting Quality Goals", *Quality Progress*, April 1988, p. 55.

Strategies for predicting future performance

Before performance can be measured, action must have taken place. Hence all performance measures have to report history. There are, however, degrees of history. Many measures, especially traditional financial ones, have limited predictive capability. The level of return on investment achieved at the end of the financial year, for example, is simply the result of a host of actions that have already taken place. Customer satisfaction today, however, may provide some insight into whether people are likely to repeat purchase tomorrow and hence what sales can be expected in the future. The relationship is not a linear one. Future sales turnover will be affected by pricing policies, competitor actions and advertising campaigns, as well as by the level of customer satisfaction achieved today. It is essential to understand the relationship, however, because customer satisfaction today is almost invariably a leading indicator of sales turnover tomorrow.

The implication of this is that it is worth hypothesising possible links between the different dimensions of performance when designing performance measures and making predictions about which indicators are leading and which are lagging. Once the measures have been introduced and data start to become available, it is feasible to begin testing which of these predictions are valid and hence constructing a model of how the business works, similar to the one shown in Figure 2.3 on page 39.

The eyes of the customer: the eyes that matter

"We measure everything that walks and moves, but nothing that matters", is how one manager recently described his organisation's measurement system to the author. Generally, people fall into the trap of measuring the things that are easy to measure. This is primarily why many businesses have hundreds of internally focused operational and financial metrics but few that capture the real needs and desires of customers. Tom Johnson, customer services director of British Telecom, illustrates the point.

The fallacy of measuring the easy things

"British Telecom used to measure how long payphones were out of order. At least, we thought that was what we were measuring. In fact, we didn't start counting a fault until a customer reported it. Most customers didn't bother to report faulty phones; they just found another one to use. It could be days before we found out that a phone was not working, and it could go wrong again half an hour after we had fixed it. None of that was visible to us."[5]

It comes down to the design of the measure. The one described above is internally focused. It measures performance from the perspective of British Telecom, not the customer. This is an easy trap to fall into. Take, for example, a measure such as delivery performance. What is on-time delivery? If a product leaves a factory on the date it is supposed to, will it be on time? Not if it is held up in shipping; or lost by the delivery company; or even delayed in the customer's in-bound warehouse. If the product arrives at the customer's site on the day it is supposed to, is it on time? Not if the customer is running a just-in-time delivery system, where each supplier is given a delivery window and the product arrives half an hour too late, or even half an hour too early. If the product arrives within the scheduled delivery window is it on time? Not necessarily; sales agents often negotiate delivery dates and times with customers. The customer may, for example, have originally requested delivery between 3.00pm and 3.30pm on Tuesday, but accepted delivery between 8.00am and 8.30am on Thursday. Even if the Thursday delivery window is achieved, the product can still be classed as late because it was not delivered at the time the customer originally wanted it.

The key issue is that of focus. People generally adopt internally focused definitions of performance, either because this makes measurement easier, or because they fail to view the process through the eyes of the customer. The result can be disastrous, because the business can quite simply fail to understand the real level of performance being achieved in the eyes of the customer. For the purposes of business performance the eyes of the customer are the only eyes that matter.

Measuring through the eyes of the customer

Constructing performance measures that reflect the way the customer sees the operation is comparatively easy, providing the designer of the measure adopts a different perspective. The key is thinking as a customer and looking at the organisation as the customers do while they are being processed. In fast food restaurants, for example, the critical dimensions of service delivery are:

- arrival
- queuing
- greeting
- ordering
- receiving food
- finding a seat
- consuming the food
- disposing of the waste
- leaving the restaurant.

Viewing the operation in this way makes it easier to establish which dimensions of performance should be measured.

Obsolete measures

Few organisations actively manage the evolution of their measurement systems. New measures are introduced in response to customer demands, management needs and performance problems. Obsolete measures are rarely deleted. Asking a simple question – is this measure useful? – can be enormously powerful, as the contrast between the companies in the following examples demonstrates.

Identifying the obsolete

In the course of a conversation the author was having with the production director of a small manufacturing company a secretary came in with a 200-page performance report. Once she had left the production director picked up the report and threw it into the bin. When asked why, he explained that the report simply summarised last week's absenteeism figures, when what he needed was information to help him manage the business now. Reporting absenteeism figures was a useful exercise for the company in the 1970s, but it has not been since the mid-1980s, and yet the company was still doing it.

Some organisations systematically manage the portfolio of measures they use. Various companies, for example, conduct an annual review of what they are measuring by asking themselves: why are we measuring this? If no reasonable answer to this question can be found, the obsolete measures are deleted from the reporting system. An alternative strategy is simply to stop issuing certain performance reports. If no one complains, then it is fair to assume that the performance report is not needed and the computer generating them can be reprogrammed.

Aligning measures and strategy

For most organisations, perhaps the most serious problem is that their measures are rarely aligned and integrated, either with each other or with the business's strategy. A recent survey of UK manufacturing firms found that of 112 managers who claimed that their firm competed on the basis of price, only 30% said that performance measures related to price were the ones to which they paid most attention.[6]

This mismatch between strategy and measures appears to be rife. Robb Dixon, professor of administrative sciences at Boston University, and his colleagues have developed a performance measurement questionnaire (PMQ) which can be used to expose the extent of this problem (see Figure 2.5).[7] The questionnaire consists of three stages. First, general data on both the company and respondent are collected. Second, the respondent is asked to identify areas of improvement that are of long-term importance to the firm and to say whether the current performance measurement system inhibits or supports appropriate activity. Third, the respondent is asked to compare and contrast what is currently most

Extract from the PMQ

Long-run importance of improvement	PERFORMANCE MEASUREMENT QUESTIONNAIRE	Effect of current performance measures on improvement
None ⊞⟶ Great	Improvement areas	Inhibit ⊞⟶ Support
1 2 3 4 5 6 7	Quality	1 2 3 4 5 6 7
1 2 3 4 5 6 7	Labour efficiency	1 2 3 4 5 6 7
1 2 3 4 5 6 7	Machine efficiency	1 2 3 4 5 6 7
1 2 3 4 5 6 7	New product introduction	1 2 3 4 5 6 7
1 2 3 4 5 6 7	Volume flexibility	1 2 3 4 5 6 7
1 2 3 4 5 6 7	Product mix flexibility	1 2 3 4 5 6 7
1 2 3 4 5 6 7	Product technology	1 2 3 4 5 6 7
1 2 3 4 5 6 7	Process technology	1 2 3 4 5 6 7
1 2 3 4 5 6 7	Manufacturing throughput times	1 2 3 4 5 6 7
1 2 3 4 5 6 7	Integration with suppliers	1 2 3 4 5 6 7
1 2 3 4 5 6 7	Integration with customers	1 2 3 4 5 6 7
1 2 3 4 5 6 7	Information systems	1 2 3 4 5 6 7
1 2 3 4 5 6 7	Direct cost reduction	1 2 3 4 5 6 7
1 2 3 4 5 6 7	Overhead cost reduction	1 2 3 4 5 6 7
1 2 3 4 5 6 7	Inventory management	1 2 3 4 5 6 7
1 2 3 4 5 6 7	Job responsibilities	1 2 3 4 5 6 7
1 2 3 4 5 6 7	Performance measurement	1 2 3 4 5 6 7
1 2 3 4 5 6 7	Customer satisfaction	1 2 3 4 5 6 7
1 2 3 4 5 6 7	Environmental control	1 2 3 4 5 6 7
1 2 3 4 5 6 7	Manufacturing strategy	1 2 3 4 5 6 7
1 2 3 4 5 6 7	Procurement practices	1 2 3 4 5 6 7
1 2 3 4 5 6 7	Offshore manufacturing	1 2 3 4 5 6 7
1 2 3 4 5 6 7	Computer integrated manufacturing (CIM)	1 2 3 4 5 6 7
1 2 3 4 5 6 7	Education and training	1 2 3 4 5 6 7

Source: Dixon, J.R., Nanni, A.J., and Vollman, T.E., *The New Performance Challenge – Measuring Operations for World-Class Competition*, Dow Jones-Irwin, Homewood, IL, 1990.

Gaps and false alarms identified by the PMQ `2.6`

STRATEGIC ACTION AREAS IMPORTANCE OF IMPROVEMENT MINUS SUPPORT FOR IMPROVEMENT	
Gaps Top quartile	False alarms Bottom quartile
New product introduction	Inventory management
Product technology	Machine efficiency
Overhead cost reduction	Labour efficiency
Integration with suppliers	Environmental control
Performance measurement	Offshore manufacturing
Information systems	Direct cost reduction

important for the firm with what the measurement system emphasises.

Data are collected using seven-point Likert scales (strongly agree to strongly disagree), then four types of analysis are conducted.

1 Alignment analysis, which assesses the extent of match between the firm's strategies, actions and measures (see Figure 2.6).
2 Congruence analysis, which provides more detail on the extent to which the strategies, actions and measures are mutually supportive.
3 Consensus analysis, where the data are analysed according to management position or function.
4 Confusion analysis, where the range of responses, and hence the level of disagreement, is examined.

Another question often worth asking when conducting performance measurement questionnaire analyses centres on the effectiveness of the performance measures currently being used. How effective is this measure? That is, does it provide valid information? The reason for asking this question is that if ineffective measures are being used to monitor progress, performance may appear to be improving, or worsening, even when it is not. This problem is particularly acute when it comes to priority improvement areas as it can result in corrective action not being taken when it should be and vice versa.

Figure 2.7 on the next page shows an extract from a modified performance measurement questionnaire, which the author and his colleagues used to conduct an analysis of the performance measurement systems in use at a major manufacturer of writing instruments.[8]

2.7

A modified PMQ

	Relative to available management time, how important is it that performance improves in terms of... None → Great	How much emphasis do you think is placed on the measurement of... None → Great	Effective performance measures provide useful information. How effective are your performance measures of... None → Great
Profit	1 2 3 4 5 DK*	1 2 3 4 5 DK	1 2 3 4 5 DK
Cost of dispatches	1 2 3 4 5 DK	1 2 3 4 5 DK	1 2 3 4 5 DK
Cost of goods sold	1 2 3 4 5 DK	1 2 3 4 5 DK	1 2 3 4 5 DK
Earnings per £ of sales	1 2 3 4 5 DK	1 2 3 4 5 DK	1 2 3 4 5 DK
Value of invoiced sales	1 2 3 4 5 DK	1 2 3 4 5 DK	1 2 3 4 5 DK
Labour efficiency	1 2 3 4 5 DK	1 2 3 4 5 DK	1 2 3 4 5 DK
Direct labour cost	1 2 3 4 5 DK	1 2 3 4 5 DK	1 2 3 4 5 DK
Indirect labour cost	1 2 3 4 5 DK	1 2 3 4 5 DK	1 2 3 4 5 DK
Direct labour hours	1 2 3 4 5 DK	1 2 3 4 5 DK	1 2 3 4 5 DK
Indirect labour hours	1 2 3 4 5 DK	1 2 3 4 5 DK	1 2 3 4 5 DK
Material usage	1 2 3 4 5 DK	1 2 3 4 5 DK	1 2 3 4 5 DK
Overhead recovery	1 2 3 4 5 DK	1 2 3 4 5 DK	1 2 3 4 5 DK
Fixed cost recovery	1 2 3 4 5 DK	1 2 3 4 5 DK	1 2 3 4 5 DK
Sales turnover	1 2 3 4 5 DK	1 2 3 4 5 DK	1 2 3 4 5 DK

*If you do not know the answer to a particular question please circle DK (don't know).

Managers' perceptions of priority improvement areas — 2.8

PERFORMANCE MEASURE

- Customer satisfaction
- Sales turnover
- Actual sales versus last year
- Market share
- Value of orders received
- Return on investment
- Stock-keeping units rationalisation
- New product sales
- Lead time reduction
- New product introduction time
- Value of sales this period

NOT IMPORTANT | SOMEWHAT IMPORTANT | IMPORTANT | VERY IMPORTANT | EXTREMELY IMPORTANT

.... Senior management   ——— Level 2   ——— Level 3   ■ ■ ■ ■ Overall

Representatives from three levels of management and four functional areas completed the questionnaire. The analysis that followed resulted in some valuable insights.

- Significant differences existed across the management hierarchy in terms of people's perception about priority improvement areas (see Figures 2.8, 2.9 and 2.10).
- Significant differences existed across the different functions in respect of priority improvement areas (see Figure 2.11).
- Significant concerns were expressed about some of the measures used to assess performance improvement in priority areas (see Figure 2.12).

The performance measurement questionnaire is a simple tool and an easy one to apply, but as can be seen from Figures 2.8–2.12, the data it generates provide deep and valuable insights into the strengths and weaknesses of an organisation's measurement system.

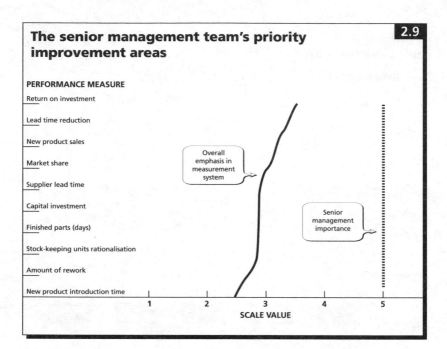

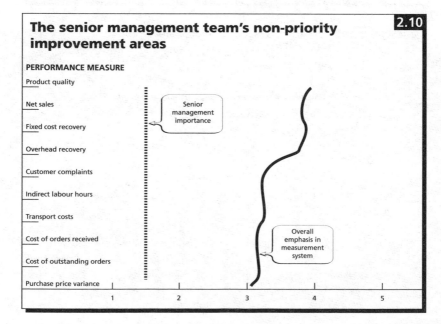

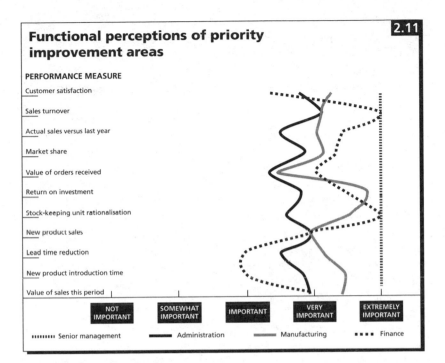

Functional perceptions of priority improvement areas

`2.11`

PERFORMANCE MEASURE

- Customer satisfaction
- Sales turnover
- Actual sales versus last year
- Market share
- Value of orders received
- Return on investment
- Stock-keeping unit rationalisation
- New product sales
- Lead time reduction
- New product introduction time
- Value of sales this period

| NOT IMPORTANT | SOMEWHAT IMPORTANT | IMPORTANT | VERY IMPORTANT | EXTREMELY IMPORTANT |

Senior management · · · · · · · · Administration ── Manufacturing ── Finance ▪ ▪ ▪ ▪

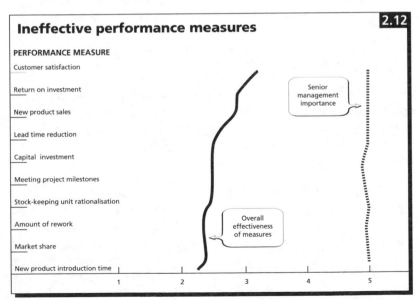

Ineffective performance measures

`2.12`

PERFORMANCE MEASURE

- Customer satisfaction
- Return on investment
- New product sales
- Lead time reduction
- Capital investment
- Meeting project milestones
- Stock-keeping unit rationalisation
- Amount of rework
- Market share
- New product introduction time

Senior management importance

Overall effectiveness of measures

1   2   3   4   5

The need for performance managers

Most organisations have many of the basic building blocks in place for an excellent performance measurement system. Often the problem is that they have not managed to integrate their measures – top to bottom, left to right. There are several reasons for this, but one of the most important is that few organisations employ people specifically to manage the performance measurement system. It is common for a business to have a surfeit of accountants reporting on financial performance, but few or even no performance managers. Yet the role of the performance manager is at least as important as that of the accountant.

The lack of performance managers often results in measurement anarchy. Many organisations have duplicate measures, with different people measuring the same dimension of performance, but in slightly different ways. For example, a sales manager may be receiving lots of complaints about late deliveries, and yet the production manager has data to prove that 97% of orders have been dispatched on time. The explanation for the conflict is that each is using a different yardstick. The sales manager is measuring on-time delivery to the day, the production manager to the week.

So some of the problems with the measurement systems of today are:

- an excessive focus on operational and financial measures, the majority of which are tactical and merely report history;
- a tendency to measure too much, which often results in the wrong things being measured because they are easy to measure; and
- a lack of integration between measures and strategy.

These problems are not new. In 1908 W. Hamilton Church observed that businesses were measuring the wrong things when he said: "Shop charges (overheads) frequently amount to 100%, 125%, and even much more of the direct wages. It is therefore actually more important that they should be correct than that the actual wage costs should be correct."[9]

The changes behind business performance measurement

What makes these problems so acute today? Why is there so much focus on business performance measurement? It is impossible to answer this question definitively, but evidence suggests that there are seven main reasons:

- the changing nature of work;
- increasing competition;

- specific improvement initiatives;
- national and international quality awards;
- changing organisational roles;
- changing external demands; and
- the power of information technology.

The changing nature of work

Traditional accounting systems allocate overheads on the basis of direct labour. In the 1950s and 1960s this was appropriate because direct labour often constituted more than 50% of the cost of goods sold. By the 1980s, however, direct labour rarely constituted more than 5–10% of the cost of goods sold, because of the massive investments that had been made in process automation. The net effect of this was that allocating overheads on the basis of direct labour resulted in wildly erroneous product costs, which in turn meant that managers made the wrong decisions.[10,11]

These arguments were so widely and vocally publicised that they resulted in the development of alternative methods of product costing, most notably activity-based costing[12] and throughput accounting[13]. During the late 1980s and early 1990s most of the major consulting companies were selling services based on these new methods of costing. The associated marketing programmes, and the popularity of books such as *Relevance Lost*,[14] meant that few in business could avoid being exposed to the message that the assumptions underpinning the traditional methods of cost accounting were fundamentally flawed, given today's operating environment.

H. Thomas Johnson, co-author of *Relevance Lost*, attributes the severity of this problem to the desire for "management by remote control". He suggests that before the 1950s financial measures of performance were used primarily as a means of planning, rather than control. As the transport and communication infrastructures developed and industries consolidated, organisations grew in size, scope and complexity. Senior managers were forced to look for practical ways of managing diverse enterprises and they settled on financial measures as the best way of doing this. Managers of business units responded by concentrating on financial performance, investing in technology, reducing head count, sweating assets and maximising return on investment. In the post-war years this was a tenable strategy because market demand generally exceeded capacity. By the 1970s, however, the dynamics of the market place, and of the organisations themselves, had changed, and internally focused, financially biased measurement systems began to show their flaws.

Increasing competition
There can be little doubt that the level of competition organisations face is increasing on a global basis. Businesses throughout the world are under continual pressure to reduce costs and enhance the value they deliver to their customers. British Telecom, for example, has shed 120,000 jobs since 1989. Many of the resultant cost savings have been passed on to customers in the form of price cuts, which have been made necessary by the deregulation of the UK telecommunications market. The European Commission's open skies policy means that for the first time cut-price carriers, such as Easy Jet and Virgin, are able to offer flights between any two destinations they choose (assuming they can negotiate the necessary take-off and landing slots). Manufacturing businesses, such as Toyota, have revolutionised the way people think about operations through their search for greater efficiency and effectiveness. The widespread acceptance of so-called Japanese manufacturing practices demonstrates how successful they have been, but the net effect is a continual rise in global performance standards and customer expectations, which in turn lead to ever greater levels of competition.

These changes have affected performance measurement in three ways. First, many organisations now actively seek to differentiate themselves from their competitors in terms of quality of service, flexibility, customisation, innovation and rapid response. They have been forced to do so because they find themselves competing in markets where value, rather than cost, is the primary driver. Competing on the basis of non-financial factors means that these organisations need information on how well they are performing across a broad range of dimensions. If a company bases its strategy on its ability to customise products, then knowing whether it really is customising products, and whether it is customising them rapidly and cheaply enough, is essential. The traditional measures used to assess business performance simply do not provide this insight. Hence organisations have been forced to change their measures because they have changed their strategies.

Second, in doing so many organisations have realised one of the hidden benefits of matching measures and strategies: that performance measures can encourage the implementation of strategy. It is widely accepted that performance measures influence behaviour. Evidence of this is seen in the academic obsession with referred journal papers. Indeed, the UK's Research Assessment Exercise provides an excellent example of how performance measures can modify behaviours on a mass scale. In 1992 the first Research Assessment Exercise was conducted. The performance of all higher education institutes was assessed in various areas. One criterion used was research excellence, which in turn was measured in terms of the number of publications per research-active member of staff. Different institutions adopted different strategies to boost their scores. Some recruited prolific publishers. Others chose to register only a small proportion of their faculty as research active.

The exercise was repeated in 1996. In the intervening years the number of publication outlets appears to have grown exponentially. Whether by accident or design, the 1992 Research Assessment Exercise had the desired effect. It encouraged academics to disseminate their work. For the 1996 Research Assessment Exercise the criteria were changed and the emphasis was put on quality, rather than quantity, of publications. Hence everyone was asked to submit details of their best three publications. The message that this changed performance measure sent was: "You have shown us that you can disseminate your work; now prove that you can disseminate high-quality work."

The link to strategy is subtle, but powerful. Measures that are aligned with strategy not only provide information on whether the strategy is being implemented, but also encourage behaviours consistent with the strategy. Henry Mintzberg has long argued that the strategy an organisation realises is a function of the pattern of decisions and actions it takes.[15] Plant location, supplier policies, incentive schemes, employment practices, marketing campaigns and a host of other decisions affect an organisation's realised strategy. When Nissan opened its first manufacturing plant in the UK its intended business strategy was "to build profitably the highest-quality car in Europe". If the purchasing manager at Nissan had independently decided to buy low-cost, low-quality components, then Nissan could have found itself realising a radically different strategy to the one it had planned to adopt. If Nissan's purchasing performance measures had emphasised the importance of cost over quality this could well have been the outcome. This is a simple example, but it illustrates the point that inappropriately designed performance measures can hinder the implementation of strategy, just as appropriately designed ones can encourage it.

Third is the fashion there has been for downsizing. Most organisations have slimmed down by eliminating middle management and empowering the remaining employees. Anecdotal evidence suggests that empowering people can be highly effective, but only if such people know the overall direction in which the business is heading. Middle managers used to ensure that this was the case by translating strategic plans into operational targets, monitoring progress and generally co-ordinating the efforts and activities of their subordinates. Today few organisations find themselves with sufficient human capacity to operate in this way. Hence they need new ways of communicating to their employees where the business is heading. Business performance measures provide one such means of communication. Just as with the Research Assessment Exercise described earlier, leading organisations are using their measurement systems as a means of communicating to their employees what is important.

Specific improvement initiatives
In response to increased competition, numerous organisations have embarked upon specific improvement initiatives. Some of these have come and gone, although most have been swept up into generic themes, such as total quality management (TQM), lean production and world class manufacturing (WCM). Few would dispute that, of these, TQM has been one of the most pervasive. Open any text on this topic and you will find discussions of continuous improvement, Deming (plan-do-check-act) cycles, statistical process control, Taguchi methods and quality costing. All these tools and techniques have one thing in common: they rely on performance measurement. The essence of continuous improvement, for example, is to seek constantly ways in which products and processes can be improved, so that greater value can be delivered to customers at ever-greater levels of efficiency. Before any organisation can determine what it needs to improve, however, it has to establish where and why its current performance falls short. Hence the need for performance measures.

Similar arguments apply to statistical process control. Control charts provide a means of checking whether processes, generally repetitive manufacturing processes, are under control; in other words, whether the outputs they are producing vary only as much as would be expected, given the norms of statistical variation. Answering this question requires performance data to be collected. Without these data statistical process control quite simply cannot be introduced.

TQM is not the only specific improvement initiative to have put performance measurement on the agenda. The widespread business interest in benchmarking has been another important driver. Xerox, largely through the efforts of Bob Camp, has been particularly vocal on this topic.[16] The rapid emergence of benchmarking clubs and a number of high-profile research studies, such as the *The Lean Enterprise Benchmarking Project*[17] and *Made in Europe*[18] studies have also

Lean enterprise benchmarking data 2.13

PRODUCT WORLD CLASS COMPARISONS

Summary average product data across plants	Seats	Exhausts	Brakes
Units per labour hour[1]	0.84	5.31	9.32
Customer complaints (parts per million – ppm)[2]	1,739	1,131	116
Sales ($)[3]	$95.1m	$60.3m	$70.5m
Price per unit ($)	$548.34	$43.70	$27.00
Materials (% of cost)	81.8%	61.3%	65.1%
Direct labour (% of cost)	5.2%	11.2%	9.2%
Annual production volume (units)	174,000	1,815,442	2,787,120
Total headcount (direct and indirect)[4]	240	352	302
Assembly automation (%)	8.1%	36.5%	55.9%
Stock turns per year	89.0	34.5	31.3
Number of car assembly plants supplied	1 to 2	7 to 8	11 to 12
Frequency of delivery to customers	every 1.5 hrs	every 36 hrs	every 46 hrs
Total number of plants	33	18	20

Source: Andersen Consulting, *Worldwide Manufacturing Competitiveness Study: The Second Lean Enterprise Benchmarking Report*, London, 1994.

1 Units per hour was calculated by taking the volume of output (in units) over a period of 12 months and dividing it by the labour hours for the same period. In the case of exhaust plants, an adjustment was made for product complexity, according to the number of component parts per piece. Labour hours covered operators, team leaders, supervisors and materials handlers, and included overtime. Vacations, break times and time lost through absenteeism were deducted. An adjustment was made for vertical integration (the amount of work contracted out).

2 The main quality measure was the number of units which the plant's customers (the car assemblers) had claimed were defective during the 12-month period covered by the study. This was expressed in parts per million (ppm) as a proportion of the volume of output produced during the same period.

3 All monies are in US dollars. Currency conversions were based on average exchange rates for 1993, at the rate of US$1 to C$1.30; FFr5.68; DM1.67; L1,570.48; ¥112.08; 3.14 pesos; Pta126.95; £0.66.

4 Total headcount includes all the group in note 2 plus indirect support functions such as maintenance, finance, quality, personnel, engineering, dispatch and distribution, etc.

heightened industrial interest. In essence, however, benchmarking studies, especially those which compare performance rather than practice, are effectively structured applications of business performance measurement. Data summarising the performance of different businesses are gathered and compared. Performance gaps, performance shortfalls and even performance advantages are identified. Such studies are valuable precisely because they provide rich performance insights (see Figure 2.13).

These insights often result in organisations realising that they need to achieve radical performance improvements merely to survive, let alone to prosper. One method for achieving these is business process re-engineering. Instead of seeking to optimise the efficiency of each operation within each function, business process re-engineering calls for the horizontal flows of information and materials to be considered as a whole when seeking performance improvements. This relies on a clear understanding of the impact of the outputs of one micro process on the next micro process, which in turn requires data to be fed back from the receiving process to the supplying process. Few organisations have measurement systems which allow this to happen, and rarely are the traditional measures of business performance appropriate. Measures such as labour utilisation, for example, might provide some insight into how efficiently a process is running, but give no indication of the impact of the outputs of one process on the next process in terms of quality and time. One of the first things organisations realise when they begin to re-engineer their processes is that once they have done so they will have to re-engineer their measurement systems.

The underlying theme is that a fundamental shift is taking place in business. Organisations have transcended their cost phase and entered a value phase. Businesses today operate in an environment where value is paramount. They have to strive continuously to deliver products and services of ever-greater value to their customers, often at ever-lower costs. To do so, they have been forced to adopt a variety of performance improvement programmes, the vast majority of which demand that they upgrade their business performance measurement systems.

National and internal quality awards

In recognition of the substantial improvements in business performance that many organisations have achieved, a number of national and international quality awards have been established. One of the first was the Deming Prize, which was introduced in Japan in 1950. Given W. Edwards Deming's pre-eminence in the field of quality management it is little wonder that this award is made by the Japanese Union of Scientists and Engineers (JUSE) for "contribution to quality and dependability of products".

Of the numerous other quality awards that have since been introduced, the highest profile are the Baldridge Award in the United States and the European Foundation for Quality Management (EFQM) Award. The popularity of such awards is illustrated by the fact that there are over 385,000 references to the EFQM award on the World Wide Web. Each of these awards requires firms to complete a comprehensive self-assessment as part of the application process. To apply for the Deming Prize, for example, organisations have to submit detailed information, as indicated below.

Extract from the Deming Prize Guide for Overseas Companies, 1996

Policies
- Quality and quality control policies and their place in overall business management
- Clarity of policies (targets and priority measures)
- Methods and processes for establishing policies
- Relationship of policies to long- and short-term plans
- Communication (deployment) of policies, and grasp and management of achieving policies
- Executives' and managers' leadership

Organisation
- Appropriateness of the organisational structure for quality control and status of employee involvement
- Clarity of authority and responsibility
- Status of interdepartmental co-ordination
- Status of committee and project team activities
- Status of staff activities
- Relationships with associated companies (group companies, vendors, contractors, sales companies, and so on)

Information
- Appropriateness of collecting and communicating external information
- Appropriateness of collecting and communicating internal information
- Status of applying statistical techniques to data analysis
- Appropriateness of information retention
- Status of utilising information
- Status of utilising computers for data processing

Standardisation
- Appropriateness of the system of standards
- Procedures for establishing, revising and abolishing standards
- Actual performance in establishing, revising and abolishing standards
- Contents of standards
- Status of utilising and adhering to standards
- Status of systematically developing, accumulating, handing down and utilising technologies

Human resources
- Education and training plans and their development and results
- Status of quality consciousness, consciousness of managing jobs, and understanding of quality control
- Status of supporting and motivating self-development and self-realisation
- Status of understanding and utilising statistical concepts and methods
- Status of quality control circle development and improvement suggestions
- Status of supporting the development of human resources in associated companies

Quality assurance
- Status of managing the quality assurance activities system
- Status of quality control diagnosis
- Status of new product and technology development (including quality analysis, quality deployment and design review activities)
- Status of process control
- Status of process analysis and process improvement (including process capability studies)
- Status of inspection, quality evaluation and quality audit
- Status of managing production equipment, measuring instruments and vendors
- Status of packaging, storage, transport, sales and service activities
- Responding to product usage, disposal, recovery and recycling
- Status of quality assurance
- Status of customer satisfaction
- Status of assuring reliability, safety, product liability and environmental protection

Maintenance
- Rotation of management (PDCA) cycle control activities
- Methods for determining control items and their levels
- In-control situations (status of utilising control charts and other tools)
- Status of taking temporary and permanent measures
- Status of operating management systems for cost, quantity, delivery, etc
- Relationship of quality assurance system to other operating management systems

Improvement
- Methods of selecting themes (important activities, problems and priority issues)
- Linkage of analytical methods and intrinsic technology
- Status of utilising statistical methods for analysis
- Status of analysis results
- Status of confirming improvement results and transferring them to maintenance/control activities
- Contribution of quality control circle activities

Effects
- Tangible effects (such as quality, delivery, cost, profit, safety and environment)
- Intangible effects
- Methods for measuring and grasping effects
- Customer satisfaction and employee satisfaction
- Influence on associated companies
- Influence on local and international communities

Future plans
- Status of current situations
- Future plans for improving problems
- Projection of changes in social environment and customer requirements and future plans based on these projected changes
- Relationships among management philosophy, vision and long-term plans
- Continuity of quality control activities
- Concreteness of future plans

The implication for business performance measurement is clear. As an ever-increasing number of organisations explore the frameworks underpinning these awards, the fact that their traditional performance measurement systems are woefully inadequate becomes apparent. Organisations decide either to ignore this message or to act upon it. The evidence to date suggests that most opt to change their performance measurement systems.

Changing organisational roles
In the 1980s and 1990s there have been subtle changes in organisational roles. Many of the most vocal critics of traditional performance measurement systems have come from the academic accounting community. As the force of their arguments has gathered strength, the professional accounting associations have reacted. The Chartered Institute of Management Accountants (CIMA) and the Institute of Chartered Accountants of Scotland (ICAS) regularly organise conferences and workshops on non-financial performance measurement. The Institute of Chartered Accountants in England and Wales (ICAEW) has released a report entitled *Corporate Governance: Performance Measurement in the Digital Age*.[19] All these bodies are encouraging their members to take a more active role in the development of balanced measurement systems, arguing that the role of the management accountant is to provide the management information necessary for running a business, rather than merely the financial information required for external reporting.

There is growing evidence that this theme has been picked up by several organisations. In the mid-1990s, for example, Cable and Wireless renamed its Corporate Management Accounting Group as Group Performance Analysis and Development, when asking the group to play a more active role in the analysis of performance data.

Human resource managers are also taking a more active role in BPM. There appear to be three reasons for this. First, performance measures are often integral to performance management systems (goal setting, measurement, feedback and reward), which generally fall within the remit of the human resource function. Second, there is considerable debate on whether performance measures should be linked to reward, which is another issue concerning human resources. Lastly, many organisations have been through substantial downsizing programmes in recent years. One of the challenges such organisations face is motivating those who remain once the downsizing programme has been completed. Performance measures can help achieve this, as they help clarify performance expectations, which in turn allows more discretion to be given to individuals as the boundaries within which they have to work become more obvious.

Changing external demands
Organisations today are subject to a wide variety of external demands, each of which has implications for business performance measurement.

Deregulation in the UK's power generation, telecommunications and water industries, for example, has resulted in the establishment of various independent regulators. These regulators demand that the firms under their jurisdiction achieve certain performance standards, and they have the power to fine those which fail to do so. To enable the regulators to assess whether the required standards are being met, firms in each of these industries have to submit detailed performance statistics on a regular basis. For example, British Telecom has to release performance data on its quality of service and pricing policies to Oftel, the telecommunications industry regulator; and Thames Water has to release performance data on, among other things, the volume of water lost through leaks to the water industry regulator.

As these data are in the public domain and of general interest, they are monitored closely by the national press. Thames Water, for example, has been severely criticised for failing to reduce the amount of water lost through leaks in the Greater London area. To counter the resulting negative publicity, the company has started to advertise its achievements on billboards in the London underground. In terms of business performance measurement, the impact of these changes is twofold. First, the demands of the industry regulator can result in firms introducing new measures of performance so that the necessary data can be collected. Second, the scrutiny of the regulator forces firms to take certain measures seriously, thereby ensuring a strong emphasis on business performance measurement in the firm.

Legally constituted bodies such as regulators are not the only groups to put pressure on firms. Consumer magazines, such as *Which?* and *Consumer Reports*, regularly publish performance evaluations of different products and services. Even groups with limited resources can have a big impact on a company's reputation. Take, for example, a libel case involving McDonald's. Supporters of the two people taken to court by McDonald's established a web site listing the company's alleged misdemeanours. Some 21,000 files, including a copy of the leaflet that originally sparked the libel action, are available at this site, which had been accessed more than 13m times between February 1996 and May 1998.

These examples highlight the fact that information is easy to collate and disseminate, especially through the Internet. Thus monitoring and managing public opinion becomes critical for high-profile businesses.

However, public opinion is not the only thing that firms have to monitor. As already discussed, most businesses are now competing in an environment where value, not price, is the principal driver. In these circumstances ensuring that value is delivered to customers becomes crucial, which is one of the main reasons the use of customer opinion surveys has become so widespread.

Some customers not only expect high levels of service; they also expect firms to operate in specific ways. The extent to which customers can influence the way their suppliers work is a function of many factors, an important one being power. Ford, for example, has used its power as a major purchaser of automotive components to demand that its accredited suppliers introduce a scheme known as Ford QOS (Quality Operating System). The essence of the Ford quality operating system is a simple but highly effective visualisation which encourages people reviewing performance to move beyond a review of past trends and on to a discussion of action plans (see Figure 2.14). A single sheet of A4 paper is split into four quadrants. In the first the trend chart is presented. In the second analysis is carried out in an attempt to identify the root causes of the performance shortfall. In the third action plans are proposed. In the fourth the impact of implementation is monitored. The value of this visualisation is that it forces people at all levels in organisations to be explicit about their action plans and allows others to check whether the action plans are delivering the predicted benefits.

Another group putting pressure on organisations to think about what they measure and how they measure it is the financial community. Contrary to what many believe, institutional investors are interested in much more than short-term financial performance. The Association for Investment Management and Research (AIMR), a professional body representing American chartered financial analysts, published a position paper in 1993 which stated: "For financial analysts to make sound judgments and draw rational conclusions, they must judge the performance of individual business enterprises ... To do so, they need information of two types. First, management should explicitly describe its strategies, plans, and expectations."[20] A 1997 survey conducted by the Financial Executives Research Foundation (FERF) found that "investors, analysts, and other users of financial reports would find value in more extensive disclosure of the company's market and competitive position, management goals and objectives, and business segment data".[21]

The power of information technology
The last driver in the performance measurement revolution is undoubtedly the power of information technology. Not only has this made the capture and analysis of data far easier, but it has also opened

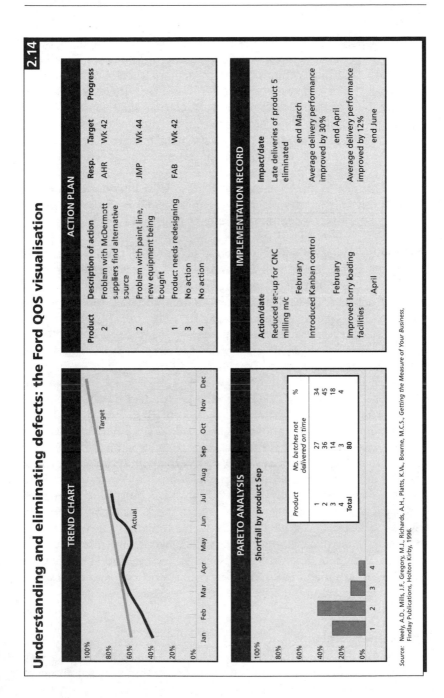

Understanding and eliminating defects: the Ford QOS visualisation

2.14

TREND CHART

ACTION PLAN

Product	Description of action	Resp.	Target	Progress
2	Problem with McDermott suppliers find alternative source	AHR	Wk 42	
2	Problem with paint line, new equipment being bought	JMP	Wk 44	
1	Product needs redesigning	FAB	Wk 42	
3	No action			
4	No action			

PARETO ANALYSIS

Shortfall by product Sep

Product	No. batches not delivered on time	%
1	27	34
2	36	45
3	14	18
4	3	4
Total	**80**	

IMPLEMENTATION RECORD

Action/date	Impact/date
Reduced set-up for CNC milling m/c	Late deliveries of product 5 eliminated
February	end March
Introduced Kanban control	Average delivery performance improved by 30%
February	end April
Improved lorry loading facilities	Average delivery performance improved by 12%
April	end June

Source: Neely, A.D., Mills, J.F., Gregory, M.J., Richards, A.H., Platts, K.W., Bourne, M.C.S., *Getting the Measure of Your Business*, Findlay Publications, Holton Kirby, 1996.

up new opportunities for data review and subsequent action. Many of the major supermarkets now actively "data mine". They monitor individual, or family spending patterns through their electronic point of sale (EPOS) systems and customer loyalty programmes. They use these data to predict when someone should be repeating their purchasing of particular products. They can then either pro-actively send their customers discount vouchers to encourage their repeat purchase, or monitor whether the expected repeat purchases take place, which in itself is a proxy indicator of customer loyalty.

There are also examples of organisations using computers to automate the data collection process. In the lobby of a hotel just outside Helsinki there is an open access computer terminal with a sign above saying "Your views count – please share them with us". On closer inspection it emerges that the computer is running a piece of software designed to elicit customers' views. Basically, the programme is an automated customer satisfaction questionnaire. Capturing the data in this way offers three substantial benefits. First, the customer enters the data online, so the hotel does not have to arrange (and pay for) data entry. Second, the risk of secondary keying errors is eliminated. Third, the hotel has real-time access to clients' views. At any time of the day or night the latest data can be reviewed and acted upon if necessary.

The use of information technology is not limited to data capture and analysis, as it also proves valuable in the processes of data presentation and dissemination. Organisations such as British Telecom[22] publish their customer service report (and the associated data) on the Internet as part of their marketing effort. Others such as Cognos,[23] Metapraxis[24] and Valstar[25] have built businesses supplying information technology support tools for performance measurement applications.

The growth in computing power has also had a negative impact on performance measurement, not least because it is now sometimes too easy for managers to generate performance reports. Indeed, there are some cases where the computer systems have enabled the capture of vast amounts of data, none of which is converted into valuable information. So although information technology has been beneficial, the caveat is: be sure to use the information technology to generate information rather than mere data.

The business benefit

The first two chapters have explored two main themes: the evidence that business performance measurement is on the agenda; and why business performance measurement is on the agenda. At this stage one fundamental question remains: what business benefit does business performance measurement deliver? There are two ways of answering it. The first involves looking at the direct benefits of business performance measurement. The second involves considering some of the hidden or intangible benefits.

Alan Meekings, a vice-president of Gemini Consulting, claims: "British Rail's Network SouthEast used performance indicators to help grow off-peak income by 28%, reduce controllable costs by 30%, and improve both service delivery and customer satisfaction from worst ever to best ever on record."[26] A survey conducted by American consultants Lingle and Schiemann found that:

"Organisations which are tops in their industry, stellar financial performers and adept change leaders, distinguish themselves by the following characteristics: having agreed-upon measures that managers understand; balancing financial and non-financial measurement; linking strategic measures to operational ones; updating their strategic scorecard regularly; and clearly communicating measures and progress to all employees."[27]

Similar claims are made by Andersen Consulting. Its research suggests that five key factors separate high performers from other firms, including the existence of detailed performance metrics for service costs, margins and customer behaviour, rather than raw customer satisfaction data.[28] Researchers from the University of Michigan and the Stockholm School of Economics provide further evidence. They have identified a significant positive correlation between customer satisfaction and financial performance using the Swedish Customer Satisfaction Barometer.[29] In the summary of their empirical findings, they report that an annual one-point increase in customer satisfaction has a net present value of $7.48m over five years for a typical firm in Sweden. Given their sample's average net income of $65m, this represents a cumulative increase of 11.5%. If the impact of customer satisfaction on profitability is similar for firms in the *Business Week* 1,000, then an annual one-point increase in the average firm's satisfaction index would be worth $94m or 11.4% of current return on investment (ROI).[30]

Perhaps the most exciting development, however, was Kleinwort Benson's establishment of two new investment funds in late 1996. These are based on portfolios of companies which deliver and sustain returns.

The investment model assumes a strong correlation between inclusive-type companies and better investor returns through three stages: evaluating management; assessing business processes; and the interaction of these to build shareholder value. Kleinwort Benson constructed its portfolios using a scorecard which built upon the European Foundation for Quality Management's Business Excellence Model and the UK's Investors In People programme, along with inclusive and corporate governance approaches to business. A Fundamental Evaluation Assessment, which analyses cashflow, sustainability of growth, sensitivities of financial performance and improvements in individual measurement targets, was conducted to decide which companies should be included in the portfolio. Other important parameters – price/earnings ratio, dividend yield, discounted cash flow and net asset valuations – were also examined. When aggregated these parameters helped determine the most undervalued and, therefore, attractive portfolio.

"Prior to launch, the model was tested against a sample of 350 UK companies based on market capitalisation: it outperformed them for the measures above by 16% in the short term and 38% in the longer term. Also, Kleinwort Benson calculations have revealed that a 1% change in each of sales growth, employee and supplier value added for portfolio companies, would give a 24% improvement in operating profit, a 5.3% lift to return on capital, and a 43% improvement in economic value added".[31]

Intangible benefits of business performance measurement
The less tangible benefits of business performance measurement centre on the process of developing a balanced measurement system. This process is valuable for two reasons: it provides new insights into the business; and it facilitates the act of integrating the management team. As Tony Singarayar, former director of process redesign at McNeil Consumer Products, part of Johnson & Johnson, says: "There are few today that know how to do this [build a balanced measurement system]. And fewer still that do it well. I'm not sure which is more proprietary in a scorecard – the data it contains, or the management process that went into creating it."[32]

In 1994 the author was working with the management team of an auto components supplier. The general manager had recently inherited a new management team and he felt that they needed to learn how to work together. He decided that a balanced measurement system would be valuable, and that the process of developing it might help the team members understand each other's functional roles. About half-way through the second meeting the manufacturing director of the business became extremely agitated. He interrupted the meeting and said: "Why are we always picking on manufacturing at this meeting? Why do we never talk about what sales and development are doing? This whole process is a waste of time. We have no clear strategy for the business. We have no clear direction and all we seem to do is criticise me and my people."

The rest of the team allowed the manufacturing director to let off steam, and when he had calmed down the meeting carried on. At the end of the session the general manager said: "Well, I think that was a productive morning and I would like to fix a date for the next session." At this point the manufacturing director decided to test the commitment of the group. He said: "I am quite happy for us to have another meeting, but I would appreciate it if we could have a meeting at a sensible time. We normally meet at 10am. I know the only reason we do this is because sales and marketing do not get in before 10am, but my day starts at 8am. So if we could meet at, say, 8.30am I would have a chance to walk round the plant, check that everything is okay. We could meet for an hour and a half to two hours and I could be back at the plant before the morning coffee break which would be a more sensible way of structuring my day." The sales and marketing director was a placid character, but by now he had had enough. So he replied: "Look, my guys have no problem coming in early. Why don't we start at 7.30am and then you can be back in the factory even earlier?"

A bidding process ensued with manufacturing finally giving in when sales made a bid for a 5.30am start. So the management team settled on 6am. No meeting in this business started on time. The general manager was one of the world's great networkers. He always had an extra phone call to make. The author and his colleague decided to arrive a few minutes before 6am, fairly secure in the knowledge that the meeting would not start on time because the general manager would have found something else to do. When they arrived at 5.50am they found the entire management team around the table. It was the most productive meeting that the author has ever been party to. Suddenly the topic had become a business issue. The commitment of every member of the senior management team had been tested and everybody had demonstrated that they really cared about the issues being discussed. This group of people had begun to work together as a team.

Should measurement be on your agenda?

The following questions provide a quick method of assessing whether an organisation's measurement system measures up. Every question can be answered either yes or no. Score 1 point for a yes and 0 points for a no. Scores of 30 or less suggest the measurement system being assessed requires urgent attention. Scores of 31–45 highlight the fact that there is room for improvement. Scores of over 45 indicate that the measurement system is in great shape.

1. Purpose of the measurement system

Our performance measurement system enables the owners of the business to:

- Assess whether the business is providing an appropriate return on their investment.
- Predict whether the business is likely to continue to be able to provide an appropriate return on their investment.

Our performance measurement system enables the directors of the business to:

- Assess how healthy the business is, that is, establish whether it is creating value at an appropriate rate.
- Understand how the business is creating this value.
- Identify strategies required to ensure that the creation of value continues.

Our performance measurement system enables the managers of the business to:

- Establish whether strategies to create value for the owners are being implemented.
- Determine whether strategies to create value for the owners are working.
- Assess whether the resources at their disposal are being used effectively (to do the right things).
- Assess whether the resources at their disposal are being used efficiently (to do things in the right way).

Our performance measurement system enables the employees to:

- Understand what the business is trying to do.
- See how well the business is performing.

- See how well they are performing.
- Identify how they can improve their performance.

Our performance measurement system enables the suppliers to:
- Understand what the business is trying to do.
- See how well the business is performing.
- See how well they are performing.
- Identify how they can improve their performance.

Our performance measurement system enables the customers to:
- Assess whether the goods and services offered by the business are better than those offered by the competition.
- Predict whether the goods and services offered by the business are likely to remain better than those offered by the competition.

2. Characteristics of the measurement system
Our performance measures are simple to understand:
- They are based upon an explicitly defined formula.
- They have visual impact.
- They are calculated using an explicitly defined source of data.
- They relate to specific, stretching, but achievable goals.
- They have an explicit purpose.
- They are reported in a simple, consistent format.

Our performance measures are efficient:
- The information provided is worth the cost of collecting the data.
- They are correct; they actually measure what they are meant to measure.
- They provide accurate feedback.
- They provide feedback in time to do something about it.
- They provide advanced warning of when something is going out of control.
- Whenever possible they use data which are automatically collected as part of a process.

Our performance measures are actionable:
- The measures can be acted upon.

Our performance measurement system is well-designed:
- It contains a mix of financial and non-financial measures.

- It contains internal (company) and external (market-focused) measures.
- It contains short-term and long-term measures.
- It does not contain too many measures.
- It contains no conflicting measures.

Our performance measurement system is robust:
- It is comprehensive.
- It does not only encourage short-term actions.

Our performance measurement system is consistent with the rest of our organisation:
- It is aligned with the incentive schemes we use.
- It takes account of our organisational structure.
- It is consistent with our manufacturing philosophy.
- It takes account of the different product families we have.
- It takes account of the fact that different products may be at different points in their life cycle.
- It takes account of the market in which we compete.

Our performance measurement system is flexible:
- It can easily be modified as circumstances change.

3. Exploitation of measures
Our performance measures:
- Are reviewed regularly.
- Actually result in action.

Our performance measurement system:
- Is reviewed regularly.
- Is updated when appropriate.

3 Why measure?

Lord Kelvin, a renowned British physicist, is reputed to have said: "When you can measure what you are speaking about, and express it in numbers, you know something about it ... [otherwise] your knowledge is of a meagre and unsatisfactory kind; it may be the beginning of knowledge, but you have scarcely in thought advanced to the stage of science." This quote is popular in measurement circles, not least because it makes clear one of the main reasons performance is measured in organisations, namely, to establish position. Managers, however, have other reasons for measuring performance: they want to know how well their business stacks up against the competition; they believe that measurement provides an equitable basis for reward; or, in some cases, they are told to measure by their boss, the owners of the business or even a regulator. There are numerous different reasons for managers to measure performance. The aim of this chapter is to review these and explore their implications.

The four CPs of measurement

Ask five different managers why they measure performance and you will receive ten different answers. Some will talk about the need to establish position. Some will emphasise that they wish to understand whether performance is improving and, if so, how rapidly it is improving. Some will claim that measures are spotlights that can be used to illuminate performance shortfalls. Others will argue that measures motivate people, or that they encourage people to modify their behaviours, and even that they can be used to communicate what is important to the organisation. Despite the diversity of opinion, however, each of the reasons offered will fall into one of four generic categories, the four CPs of measurement: check position; communicate position; confirm priorities; and compel progress.

CP1: check position

Checking position is an essential role for measurement. "You can't manage what you can't measure" is a frequently quoted homily. Knowing where you are and where you are going is crucial. Without the right measures in place everything from strategic planning to local level operational improvement becomes unreliable at best and impossible at worst. Without measures there is no way of checking whether the plans, either strategic or tactical, are appropriate or delivering the desired results. Measures provide a means of tracking position. They enable managers to monitor how performance has changed over time, and to establish whether all of the time and effort they have put in to their improvement programmes is paying off. When describing measurement systems academics and consultants talk about corporate dashboards, aeroplane cockpits and control panels. It is no accident that each of these analogies centres on the notion of a journey. Appropriate measures allow managers to track the progress of their business on its journey to excellence.

Measures as a means of establishing position
Knowing where you are and what you have to do better is essential if you want to deliver excellent customer service. FedEx effectively invented the air express package delivery business when it started operations in April 1973. By the late 1990s FedEx was handling over 3m packages a day and serving some 212 different countries in an industry worth nearly $35 billion. The future for FedEx looks bright, as the global express market is forecast to grow to $250 billion by 2015.

FedEx used to rely on a measure of on-time delivery to track customer satisfaction, but it realised that this was too narrow for a business which aspired to "satisfy worldwide demand for fast, time-definite, reliable distribution". As a result the company introduced a new measure of customer satisfaction, the service quality indicator. This consists of 12 separate measures, each of which is weighted to reflect the importance attached to it by customers. The 12 indicators and associated weightings are shown in Table 3.1.

FedEx reports service quality, which is based on the average daily figures for all 12 indicators, weekly and takes corrective action to eliminate the root causes of any frequently occurring problems. The system appears to be working. Since 1987 overall customer satisfaction with the domestic and international markets has been 95% and 94% respectively. During an independent survey of air express customers 53% of respondents gave FedEx a perfect score. Its nearest competitor achieved only 39%.[1]

Measures as a means of comparing position (benchmarking)
In the right context measures allow managers to compare, as well as establish, position. Hence the popularity of benchmarking studies, which take many forms and range from highly focused and detailed studies,

Table 3.1 **FedEx service quality indicator**

Performance dimension	FedEx weighting (points)
Right day, late service	1
Wrong day, late service	5
Traces (no. of proof of performance requests where some information cannot be located)	1
Complaints reopened by customers	5
Missing proof of delivery	1
Invoice adjustments requested	1
Missed pick-ups	10
Damaged packages	10
Lost packages	10
Over-goods (no. of packages received in over-goods – lost and found)	5
Abandoned calls	1
International (any failures on any of the above items in the international business)	1

Source: FedEx web page (http://www.fedex.com).

such as the Lean Enterprise Projects, to those that ask managers to compare their perceptions of the performance of different organisations. *Fortune,* for example, runs an annual survey to find the most admired companies in the United States. In 1997 representatives from 476 *Fortune* 1,000 companies, divided into 55 industry groups, were polled. A total of 12,600 senior executives, outside directors and financial security analysts were asked to grade the ten largest companies (or in some cases fewer) in their own industry on nine attributes of reputation:

- Quality of management
- Quality of products and services
- Innovativeness
- Investment value
- Financial soundness
- Ability to attract, develop and keep talented people
- Corporate responsibility
- Total results
- Use of assets

The scores, each on a 1–10 scale, were equally weighted and combined to give an aggregate score for every company. For the first time in 1997 all 12,600 ballot recipients were also asked which companies, regardless of industry, they admired most. Their votes determined the top ten most admired companies, which in 1997 were General Electric, Microsoft, Coca-Cola, Intel, Hewlett-Packard, Southwest Airlines, Berkshire Hathaway, Disney, Johnson & Johnson and Merck. Critics could argue that companies may be admired but this does not mean their performance is good. To resolve this issue, *Fortune* explored the stock performance of the winners. Its research showed: "If ten years ago you had bought $10,000 worth of Standard & Poor's 500 and reinvested your dividends, your estimable 17.92% annual rate of return would have compounded into $51,964 today. If you had, however, put $1,000 into each of this year's [1997] ten most admired companies, you would be sitting nearly three times prettier, with a portfolio worth $146,419."[2]

At the other end of the benchmarking spectrum the question often being asked is: which practices lead to superior organisational performance? Nick Oliver, reader in management studies at the University of Cambridge, and his team collect specific performance data from tightly defined industrial groupings in an attempt to answer this question. In studies of the automotive components industry they have investigated quality and productivity in 78 seat, exhaust, brake and wire harness manufacturing plants around the world (China, France, Germany, Italy, Japan, Spain, the UK and the United States). Their aim is to identify why some plants are able simultaneously to achieve high levels of productivity and quality but others are not. The latest findings from their research suggest the following.

- World-class plants are able to achieve a 2:1 performance differential over a range of measures, including productivity, inventories and schedule variations.
- The gap in quality is wider: 9:1 in seats and 170:1 in exhausts.
- The high performers maintain tight discipline and control over their internal processes.

To enhance the validity of the comparisons, and hence the findings, it was decided to sacrifice breadth, in terms of industry sectors covered, and maximise depth, in terms of quality of data collected.[3]

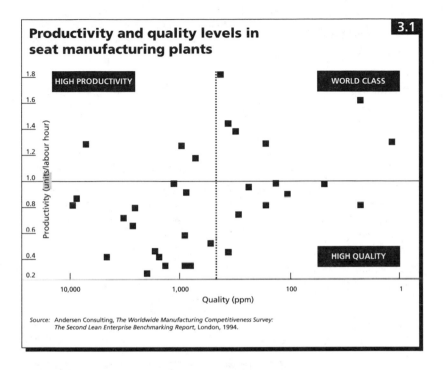

Productivity and quality levels in seat manufacturing plants

3.1

Source: Andersen Consulting, *The Worldwide Manufacturing Competitiveness Survey: The Second Lean Enterprise Benchmarking Report*, London, 1994.

Measures to monitor progress

Measures provide not only a means of establishing position, but also a method for monitoring progress. The UK's use of school league tables is an example. The performance of all schools in the UK is now assessed on the basis of pupil performance in national examinations. Although criticised for failing to consider the quality of the student intake, the league tables provide valuable data which allow parents to monitor the performance and progress of local schools. In spite of its simplicity, this example highlights three further reasons for organisations to measure performance.

- They are told to, either by the regulator or, as is the case with schools, the government.
- They want to communicate their performance and progress, usually to shareholders or customers, but sometimes to other interested parties (the parents of customers in the case of schools).
- They want to benchmark, or others want to be able to benchmark their performance.

Tracking position: critical questions to ask

Traditionally managers have tracked position by asking two simple questions:

- How good is performance today?
- How does this compare with performance yesterday?

Hence the frequency with which this year's performance is compared with last year's. A more sophisticated approach would also involve comparing this year's performance with a budget or target. But these questions are too narrow. To really track position it is necessary to seek answers to nine different questions, which between them cover position over time (yesterday, today and tomorrow) and position from different perspectives (internal, competitors and customers); see Figure 3.2.

Critical questions when tracking position 3.2

		TIME HORIZON		
		Yesterday	Today	Tomorrow
PERSPECTIVES ON PERFORMANCE	Competitor	How well were our competitors performing?	How well are our competitors currently performing?	If our competitors contrive to improve at the rate they are what will their level of performance be?
	Customer	How well did our customers want us to perform?	How well do our customers want us to perform?	If our customers continue to increase at the rate they are what level of performance will they expect?
	Company	How well were we performing?	How well are we performing?	If we continue to improve at the rate we are what will our level of performance be?

CP2: communicate position

In many scenarios communicating position is at least as important as checking it. Sometimes organisations are legally required to communicate their position in, for example, annual financial accounts, hospital waiting lists, school league tables and regulator demands. In other situations organisations choose to communicate their position, either to interested external parties (such as customers, owners and suppliers) or to interested internal parties (such as employees and unions). There are many reasons for such communications. Internal communication is often used either as a means of thanking individuals and teams, or as a means of spurring them on to even higher levels of achievement. Externally, performance may be communicated either to market the organisation (to build brand awareness and customer loyalty) or as part of an information exchange programme (for example, through benchmarking clubs). In this regard appropriate and well-defined measures provide a language which can be used as the basis of communication.

Measures as a means of communicating performance
In the mid-1990s the UK's rail network was privatised and several regional operating companies were established. One of the many changes that resulted was an increased emphasis on customer service, reflected in the appearance at many mainline stations of performance charts, summarising the timeliness of train services. At first sight these charts suggested that the operating companies were doing an excellent job, typically reporting that over 97% of trains arrived on time. This was an important message for both customers and employees, as it emphasised the quality of service they were receiving and delivering respectively.

On closer inspection, however, it becomes apparent that the charts have been carefully designed, because a train is deemed to be on time if it arrives at its final destination within five minutes of the scheduled time. This means that a train from Aberdeen to London can be half an hour late at every station en route, but as long as it makes up the time on the last leg of its journey and arrives in London within five minutes of the scheduled time it is classified as being on time. Unfortunately, not every passenger's final destination is London. The measure is good for trying to convince people that they are receiving a good service, but a poor reflection of true customer service.

Measuring because you have to: communicating with the regulator
Regulators, official watchdogs and government agencies all demand that organisations monitor and report specific performance data. Florida Power and Light (FPL), voted the most admired gas and electric utility company in the United States by readers of *Fortune* and the only non-Japanese company to win the prestigious Deming Prize, aims to "be the preferred provider of safe, reliable, cost-effective products and services that satisfy the electricity related needs of all our customer segments".

The business serves around 7m people (half the population of Florida) in an area covering the entire eastern seaboard of Florida and the southern third of the state. Florida Power and Light last increased base charges to residential customers in 1985. In fact, a typical residential customer bill was approximately 5% lower in January 1997 than it was 12 years earlier. A 1,000 kilowatt-hour residential bill, which would have cost $83.39 in 1985, had been reduced to $78.82 by January 1997. The significance of this can be seen when noting that inflation alone caused products that cost $83.39 in 1985 to rise to $125.36 by January 1997. The reason Florida Power and Light has been able to offer these price reductions, while simultaneously increasing shareholder dividends, is that continual reductions in operation and maintenance expenses have been sought. Operation and maintenance costs were 1.30 cents per kilowatt-hour in 1996 compared with 1.82 cents per kilowatt-hour in 1990, a reduction of 29%.

Impressive though this performance is, Florida Power and Light still operates in a regulated environment and is often forced to declare specific performance data to regulators and government agencies. In 1995, for example, the company submitted an application to burn an alternative boiler fuel, Orimulsion, at its Manatee power plant. When reconsidering this application in 1997, the Florida Power Plant Sitting Board requested that Florida Power and Light collect and submit detailed performance data on the following:

- Transport of raw materials and by-products.
- Proposed reductions of nitrogen oxide and particulate matter.
- Potential impact of a spill of Orimulsion on the shallows and nursery areas of Tampa Bay.
- Funding of a vessel tracking and information system for Tampa Bay.
- The overall economic impact of FPL's proposed conditions on customer bills.

In April 1998 an administrative law judge recommended approval of Florida Power and Light's Orimulsion project, following his review of 23 volumes of transcripts, some 2,958 pages in total.[4]

Strategies for communicating performance

Most organisations have many constituencies with which they have to communicate. Shareholders and investors, employees, customers, suppliers and regulators all have different interests in organisational performance. The information to be communicated and the messages to be delivered to these communities vary widely. Among other things, shareholders want to know about financial performance and the factors that might affect future financial performance. Employees are interested to understand the organisation's vision and values and how well the firm is living up to these. Regulators want to be convinced that the organisation is achieving certain minimum threshold levels of performance.

These different dimensions of performance are communicated in different ways, often using different media. A crucial factor in determining which mode of communication should be adopted is the sensitivity of the message and the extent to which interaction is required between the person delivering the message and the person receiving it. Figure 3.3 on the next page highlights the options available and provides a useful framework for auditing whether the right media are being used to deliver particular performance messages.

CP3: confirm priorities

Performance data not only provide insight into where the business is, but they also enable members of the organisation to identify how far they are from their goal. In many ways this is tantamount to checking position, not in the sense of how far the organisation has come, but of how far the organisation has to go. Once the performance shortfall becomes apparent, action plans to close the gap can be formulated and here, once again, performance measures play a role. Take, for example, the Ford quality operating system visualisation discussed in Chapter 2. This consisted of four charts: a trend chart; an analysis chart (often pareto); an action plan; and an implementation plan. The role of the implementation plan is to monitor whether the planned actions have had their

3.3

Which media for which messages?

→ Greater need for interaction

	WORLD WIDE WEB	PAPER BASED (eg, reports, newsletter)	DISCUSSION BASED (eg, meetings, video conferences)
Characteristics of media	Low interaction, limited need for follow-up action once information has been communicated. Person who wants interaction visits the web page.	Medium level of interaction. Reports/publications distributed to interested parties, often in an attempt to engage them.	High interaction. Aim is to influence perception and/or encourage action.
Typical applications	General facts and figures about the organisation. Often the data are non-controversial. Open access. Anyone interested can visit the web page.	Variety of forms of data. Annual reports produced for external consumption through to internal performance reports.	Performance reviews and performance planning sessions. Aim is to establish what to do next.
Why chosen media are appropriate	Generally, information being disclosed is non-sensitive.	Controlled access. Information moderately sensitive.	Limited involvement, but those present are expected to engage. Most appropriate forum for establishing what to do next.

desired impact. As actions are taken performance is monitored, and if the actions have their desired impact improvements in performance should be seen, albeit with a time lag in many cases. The strength of the Ford quality operating system visualisation is that it makes this link explicit. Indeed, it highlights the role measurement data have throughout the process, from monitoring trends through to analysis and the development of action plans, and ultimately in the evaluation of whether the action plans that have been implemented have paid off. Without the measurement data there is no guarantee that appropriate action plans will be developed and no means of checking whether the proposed actions plans have their desired effect.

The power of visualisation

Despite its apparent simplicity the Ford quality operating system visualisation contains a massive amount of information to help managers identify how business performance can be enhanced. Figure 3.4 on the next page shows a completed chart measuring number of defects. The data in this chart enable the reader to establish the following.

- The total number of defects found in each quarter.
- The total number of different classes of defect found in each quarter (blue = B, red = R, yellow = Y).
- The rate at which performance is improving on a quarter-by-quarter basis.
- Why performance is improving, that is, what actions have been taken and what impact they have had on performance.
- When particular improvement activities are scheduled to be completed (target dates shown in the action plan).
- When particular improvement activities are actually completed (the black flags shown in the implementation plan highlight the fact that the activity has been completed).
- The rate of improvement activities. In quarters 2–5 one improvement action was implemented every quarter. Thereafter the rate of activity tails off rapidly.
- The relative pay-off of the different improvement activities (for example, supervisor training, completed in quarter 8, appears to have had a greater, albeit delayed impact, than operator training, completed in quarter 4).

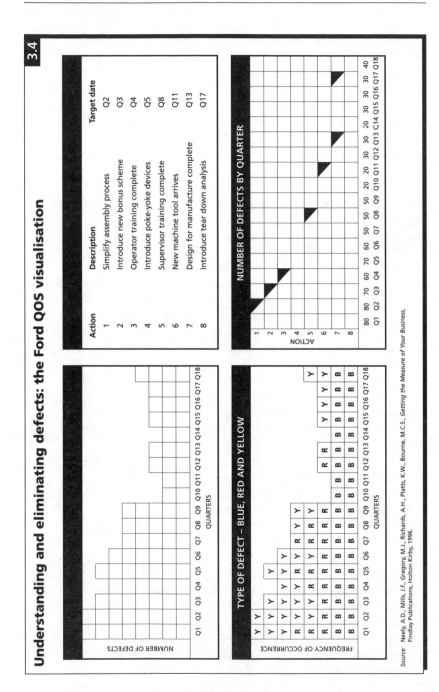

3.4

Understanding and eliminating defects: the Ford QOS visualisation

Action	Description	Target date
1	Simplify assembly process	Q2
2	Introduce new bonus scheme	Q3
3	Operator training complete	Q4
4	Introduce poke-yoke devices	Q5
5	Supervisor training complete	Q8
6	New machine tool arrives	Q11
7	Design for manufacture complete	Q13
8	Introduce tear down analysis	Q17

NUMBER OF DEFECTS BY QUARTER

TYPE OF DEFECT – BLUE, RED AND YELLOW

Source Neely, A.D., Mills, J.F., Gregory, M.J., Richards, A.H., Platts, K.W., Bourne, M.C.S, *Getting the Measure of Your Business,*
Findlay Publications, Holton Kirby, 1996.

- The fact that some improvement actions have made performance get worse (following the introduction of tear down analysis in quarter 17, for example, the number of yellow defects increased).
- Whether the improvement activities have had an impact across all dimensions of performance shortfall. (Over the course of the 18 quarters red defects have been eliminated, yellow defects have been significantly reduced, but none of the improvement actions implemented appear to have had any impact on the number of blue defects.)

Measures to manage

Many people have compared the process of measuring performance to that of an engineering control system. Take, for example, the thermostat analogy. The thermostat is set at a certain level, the desired level of performance. When the temperature in the room falls below the desired value the heating comes on. When it reaches (or exceeds) the desired value the heating is turned off. In this context measures are simply part of a mechanistic control cycle. Action is taken. Performance is measured. If progress deviates from plan then corrective action is taken. In organisational terms there are two such forms of control: cost control; and management control. Hence there are two further reasons for measuring performance: as a means of management control; and as a means of cost control.

Measures as a means of management and cost control[5]

BTR, a British industrial conglomerate with business interests in the automotive, power drives, process control and packaging and materials sectors, provides an excellent example of an organisation dedicated to using measures as a means of control. During the 1970s and 1980s the company grew at an impressive rate as a result of an aggressive acquisitions policy. Sales turnover and profit before tax increased by 25% and 31% respectively during the 1988 calendar year, and again by 26% and 29% during 1989. The 1990s have undoubtedly been more difficult for BTR, but even so the company achieved a sales turnover of £8,400m in 1996.

One of the secrets of BTR's early success was the profit planning process developed by Owen Green, the company's former chief executive (see Chapter 5 for more details), which required representatives from all divisions and business units within BTR to declare their profit targets for the following year and how they would achieve them. Underpinning the process was the notion of the three-legged stool, that is, the requirement that profit improvements have to come in roughly equal amounts from pricing changes, productivity changes, and volume and mix changes. In requiring balanced profit growth, the profit plan reduces the ability of managers to take short-term decisions which will improve next year's profitability at the expense of future years. When applied in BTR, local managers were expected to develop their own profit plans for their business units or groups. The local managing director and accountant would then meet representatives from the BTR group, who would challenge the proposed profit plan. Once agreed, the profit plan would form the basis of a financial contract between the local managing director and the BTR group. Failure to achieve the profit plan, without adequate explanation, resulted in severe sanctions, but success was always generously rewarded.

Measures to make clear

Merely using measures as a means of control, however, is short-sighted, for performance data also provide a valuable opportunity to learn. The examples of Milliken and British Telecom in Chapter 2 demonstrate how measures can be used to help the business identify the true drivers of customer satisfaction. Once these have been established it becomes possible to determine where the company is doing well and where it is not doing well, and hence what its priorities for improvement should be and where its investments should be targeted.

Measures as a means of focusing investment[6]

Mobil Oil was one of the early adopters of Kaplan and Norton's balanced scorecard.[7] Its American Marketing and Refining Division undertook a massive restructuring in 1994 in response to market pressures and the perception that the operation was nationally optimised, inwardly focused, functionally structured and carrying extremely high overheads. The company decided to decentralise and create 18 national business units, each with profit and loss accountability, and 14 service units. In doing so, however, it faced the challenge of how to remain a single business rather than splitting into 32 separate businesses. The balanced scorecard played a crucial role in helping the company address this, as it provided a common language through which the different businesses could make their needs explicit.

Mobil uses the scorecard to evaluate investment decisions as well. Instead of simply looking at financial payback, it evaluates all proposed investments against all the criteria on its agreed scorecard. Representatives from each business know that to maximise the likelihood that the investments they are proposing will be approved, they have to present a strong case, which demonstrates not only the likely returns, but also the impact of the investment on customer satisfaction, the safety of Mobil's operations, the extent to which Mobil is a good neighbour, and the degree to which Mobil's people are motivated and prepared.

CP4: compel progress

Measurement in itself will not improve performance. The impact will be observed only when people do things differently (more efficiently or effectively), or when the underlying business processes are changed. Measures can, however, compel progress in several ways.

1 Measurement communicates priorities. The relevant homilies are "tell me how you'll measure me and I'll tell you how I'll behave" and "you get what you inspect, not what you expect". The very act of measuring something sends a signal to members of the organisation which says: this is something we care about. In fact we care about it enough to invest time and effort in ensuring we constantly know how well we are doing in this performance dimension.
2 Measurement is often linked to reward. Bonus schemes are designed where individuals are paid on the basis of their performance. The measures make explicit how performance will be assessed. The bonus keeps people focused on delivering good performance versus the measures. By linking bonus payments to measures the message that particular dimensions of performance are important can be reinforced.
3 Measures make progress explicit. They provide an excellent way of checking whether the required actions have been taken and whether progress has been made. There is nothing so clear as a trend chart to establish whether particular groups, teams or sections are living up to performance expectations and requirements.

Measures as a means of motivation[8]

Motorola is one of the world's leading manufacturers and suppliers of semiconductors and electronic equipment for civil and military applications, and in 1988 it was the first American corporation to win the Baldridge Award. In the late 1970s Motorola was losing market share and ground to foreign competitors such as NEC, Toshiba and Hitachi. In response the company introduced a rigorous quality campaign, a key element of which was six sigma (6δ). According to Motorola: "Sigma is a statistical unit of measurement that describes the distribution about the mean of any process or procedure. A process or procedure that can achieve plus or minus six sigma capability can be expected to have a defect rate of no more than a few parts per million, even allowing for some shift in the mean. In statistical terms, this approaches zero defects."

Often process variability is measured in terms of ±3δ from the mean. If a process has ±3δ capability it means that on average only 1 in 400 parts will be defective. Motorola, however, makes components which can require up to 1,200 process steps, so on average any part produced is likely to have in the region of three defects (probability of any part being defective multiplied by the number of process steps). Basically, six sigma extends the odds, because processes with ±6δ capability will produce perfect work 99.9999998% of the time.

To achieve 6δ Motorola spent $25m on company-wide education in 1987. It also developed an accompanying set of standards, which required that:

- Each part of the organisation documents, installs and maintains a quality system, which explicitly identifies who is responsible for executing that unit's goal.
- Each part of the organisation adopts a formal process for planning and achieving continuous improvements in the quality and reliability of the products and services it delivers, through the permanent elimination of the root causes of any quality problems.
- Quality assurance groups in each location always act as the customer's advocate, not Motorola employees.
- Motorola establishes and maintains a corporate-wide quality council consisting of senior quality managers, for company-wide co-ordination, promotion and review of the various quality systems and programmes in place to facilitate achievement of these policies.

Through a clear and simple statement of its objectives, that is, achieve ±6δ capability by the end of 1992, a rigorous education and training programme and a robust set of standards, Motorola was able to achieve the exacting six sigma performance target. As far as the business is concerned the impact has been substantial. Defects have been cut by 80% and some $962m has been saved in inspection and rework costs alone.

Measures as a means of communicating priorities

Explicit and implicit performance measures exist in all organisations. Some years ago the author was involved in an investigation of the extent to which different managers in the same organisation shared a common view of how their organisation had chosen to compete. One of the organisations studied, a manufacturer of high-quality door and window frames, provides a useful illustration of how implicit, as well as explicit, performance measures can influence people's perceptions of priorities.

The study began with an interview with the managing director. When asked how the business had chosen to compete, he replied: "You have to understand we are a high-quality business. We produce door and window frames for high-class buildings, so the critical thing for us is that we exceed the customer's expectations in terms of product quality. We will not use wood with knots in. We will make sure our products colour match perfectly. All in all, the key driver for us is product quality."

Subsequent discussions with the production manager revealed a starkly different perception. "You have to understand", he said, "that the critical thing for us is on-time delivery. You can't have 25 builders on a site waiting for the door and window frames to arrive. We have to ensure that our product always arrives on time."

The reason for this mismatch in perceptions was that whenever the managing director spoke to the production manager he asked him about delivery performance, not product quality, which led the production manager to assume that the managing director's question – how are we doing versus schedule? – reflected his priorities. The managing director had in effect introduced an implicit performance measure through the questions he asked. This measure was driving everyone else's actions in the business and explained a spate of recent product quality complaints. So shocked was the managing director by these observations that he called an open meeting and apologised to the entire workforce for sending them the wrong messages by asking the wrong questions.

Measures as a basis for reward

There is much debate on whether pay should be linked to performance. Advocates argue that if it is not, the vast majority of people within the business have no significant incentive to strive for higher levels of performance. Doubters suggest that the basis of the reward is often so far removed from the individuals being rewarded that it is almost impossible for them to influence. Frontline staff, for example, undoubtedly affect the volume of sales made. But if there is a downturn in the market, an incentive in the form of a bonus based on the total sales turnover can be demotivating and counter-productive. To address these concerns Cigna Property & Casualty, an American-based insurance company, has introduced a two-dimensional bonus, which seeks to align individual objectives with organisational objectives and values.[9] Cigna's employees are awarded fictional shares in the business. The number of shares individuals receive is a function of their position in the organisation and their individual performance. The value of these fictional shares increases over the course of the financial year only if Cigna hits its predefined business targets. The bonus payable to each individual is calculated by multiplying these two elements together. Hence if the business has had a good year and most of the business targets have been achieved, and individuals have performed well and realised most of their personal targets, they will receive a substantial bonus. If, however, the business has performed well and individuals have not achieved their personal objectives, the bonus they receive will reflect the business's success but be moderated by the fact that they have not contributed as much as expected.

Messages from measures

Establishing whether the right messages are being communicated through the performance measurement system is critical. One way of doing this is to use the performance measurement questionnaire described in Chapter 2. Another is to identify the most important dimensions of performance, record them in a table and ask different people within the organisation to apportion 100 points among them in a way which reflects their opinion of the relative importance of each dimension. The discussion that ensues, when different people's perceptions of what is important to the business are made public, soon ensures that differences of opinion and priority are aired, debated and ideally resolved.

Multiple reasons for measuring

Perhaps the most striking thing about the preceding discussion is the number of different reasons people have for measuring performance (see "Why measure?" opposite). As noted at the beginning of the chapter, each of these reasons can be categorised under the headings: check position

(CP1); communicate position (CP2); confirm priorities (CP3); and compel progress (CP4). But the four CPS capture only one of the dimensions which explain why measurement is important to organisations. Performance measures can play a multitude of roles. Sometimes the role of measurement is to ensure compliance – to check that the organisation does not fail to meet certain minimum levels of performance. Sometimes the role is to check health – to ensure that the medium- to long-term viability of the organisation is not being threatened by the actions of competitors or the demands of customers. Sometimes the role is to allow the strategy the organisation is pursing to be challenged. These three roles of measurement (comply, check and challenge) are forgotten when the question "Why do you measure performance?" is asked because the answer – the four CPS – is obvious. When examining how measurement is used in practice, however, the importance of the three roles becomes apparent[10].

Why measure?

CP1: check position
- Measures as a means of establishing position
- Measures as a means of comparing position (benchmarking)
- Measures to monitor progress

CP2: communicate position
- Measures as a means of communicating performance
- Measuring because you have to: communicating with the regulator

CP3: confirm priorities
- Measures to manage
- Measures as a means of management and cost control
- Measures to make clear
- Measures as a means of focusing investment

CP4: compel progress
- Measures as a means of motivation
- Measures as a means of communicating priorities
- Measures as a basis for reward

4 Complying with the non-negotiable

ORGANISATIONS, like living organisms, have to satisfy certain non-negotiable performance parameters if they are to survive. A useful way to conceptualise non-negotiable performance parameters is to think of them as performance thresholds. If performance falls below the acceptable threshold the very survival of the organisation will be threatened. Take, for example, cashflow. In many ways cashflow for organisations is synonymous with oxygen for humans. If insufficient oxygen is available humans are unable to breathe, and ultimately they will die. If insufficient cash is available an organisation cannot continue to function. Investments cannot be made. Materials cannot be purchased. Employees and suppliers cannot be paid. Ultimately, organisations with insufficient cash die.

The same can be said for many other dimensions of performance, such as employee or customer satisfaction. Organisations with demotivated and frustrated employees, or which deliver poor products and services, thereby disappointing and disenfranchising their customers, ultimately will die. The critical point is that for all organisations there are certain minimum performance thresholds. Failure to exceed these thresholds can jeopardise the future of the organisation. Hence a crucial role of any organisation's measurement system is to provide an early-warning signal, which highlights the fact that the organisation is coming dangerously close to breaching one or more of the non-negotiable dimensions of performance. This role of measurement, as a means of ensuring compliance, is explored in this chapter.

The chapter has four main sections. The first provides examples of organisations that have breached some of the non-negotiable performance parameters and suffered the consequences. The second explores the notion that all the stakeholders in the organisation, rather than just the shareholders, determine which performance parameters are non-negotiable. The third presents two case studies illustrating how two particular businesses, a telecommunications operator, Nortel, and a computer services conglomerate, ICL, have tackled the question of non-negotiable performance parameters. One of the shortcomings of the strategies adopted by Nortel and ICL, and indeed by most other organisations, is that they are reactive, because the identification of potential infringements relies on an audit of performance and business practices. The fourth section reviews some alternative measurement strategies that provide more pro-active methods of ensuring that none of the non-negotiable performance parameters are breached.

Failure to comply

The most obvious examples of organisations failing to comply with non-negotiable performance parameters are provided by industrial disasters. The explosion which occurred in the fourth unit of the Chernobyl Nuclear Power Plant on April 26th 1986 is a typical example. A decade after the explosion delegates at an international conference in Vienna were still trying to piece together data which would allow the full impact of the disaster to be understood. Accounts presented at the conference suggested that reactor design faults, coupled with serious violations in safety procedures, one of which involved someone switching off the reactor protection system, resulted in:

- 28 of the 237 people who were working in the plant dying during the subsequent three months as a direct result of the radiation to which they were all exposed;
- 116,000 people being evacuated from their homes around the Chernobyl plant between April 27th and mid-August 1986;
- 210,000 people being resettled between 1990 and the end of 1995 (53,000 from Ukraine, 107,000 from Belarus and 50,000 from the Russian Federation);
- 4,300 sq km of contaminated territory being declared "an exclusion zone".

Delegates at the conference also explored the secondary impacts of the disaster. Demographic indicators showed that birth-rates in the contaminated regions had decreased significantly and that the workforce was migrating to uncontaminated regions. This had resulted in shortages of labour and professional staff. Also the attitude of the general public to products from the contaminated areas made it difficult for such products to be exported or sold locally.[1]

Hudson Foods

Hudson Foods, now part of the $8 billion Tyson Foods business, was forced to recall 25m lb of hamburger when 16 Colorado residents caught E. coli after consuming Hudson hamburgers. Using DNA fingerprinting, Colorado state investigators discovered that the patients all had the same strain of E. coli, and that this matched the strain in a sample of Hudson beef taken from one of the patient's freezers. According to Department of Agriculture officials, the most likely source for contamination was an outside slaughterhouse, but Hudson recalled its hamburgers when investigators found that the company used leftover raw meat from one day in the next day's production, potentially causing a chain of contamination.[2]

Tuta blood bags

Blood Transfusion Services in the UK were forced to destroy almost 20% of the country's blood stocks in 1995 when several bags provided by an Australian manufacturing company, Tuta, were found to have faulty heat seals, allowing the possibility of bacterial infection. Hospitals in Reading, Oxford and Southampton had to cancel several elective operations and one patient developed septicaemia after being given contaminated blood. During the crisis emergency appeals were issued for new donors and some 25,000 units of replacement blood were collected in just three days.[3]

The licence to operate[4]

Apart from the damage caused and the cost to the organisations concerned, these examples have one thing in common. They demonstrate what can happen when an organisation fails to satisfy some, or all, of its non-negotiable performance parameters. Such parameters exist in all organisations. Just as nuclear power plants cannot afford to have explosions in their reactors, food manufacturers cannot afford to give their customers food poisoning, hospitals cannot afford to use defective blood bags, express package delivery companies cannot afford to lose packages and banks cannot afford to debit accounts incorrectly if they wish to retain their respective licences to operate.

There are two important concepts here: that of non-negotiable performance parameters; and that of the licence to operate. The phrase non-negotiable performance parameters describes those dimensions of performance where the organisation has to achieve a certain minimum standard or a certain threshold level of performance if it is to survive. An analogy is that of a car's need for oil. Providing sufficient oil is available to lubricate the engine, the car will continue to operate. Excess oil adds no value and cars can be run with less than the threshold level of oil, although doing so will damage the engine. So it is with non-negotiable performance parameters. Restaurants can survive even if they give a few of their clients food poisoning. Oil companies, as Shell has demonstrated, can survive adverse publicity with respect to their environmental policies. Repeated failure to achieve the threshold level of performance, however, can damage the organisation's brand, image or reputation and ultimately result in its licence to operate being revoked.

This brings us back to the second concept: the licence to operate. All organisations have licences to operate. Not in the formal sense of pieces of paper or certificates, although these are issued in certain cases (such as the airline industry), but in the informal sense of whether people are willing to accept and deal with the organisation. Anyone who chooses to deal with an organisation is, in effect, implicitly granting that organisation a licence to operate, just as anyone who elects not to deal with a particular organisation is denying that organisation's licence to operate. At a practical level this means that all organisations are granted licences to operate by several different parties (regulators, employees, customers, suppliers), and that each of these parties can seek to revoke the organisation's licence to operate at any time.

Examples to illustrate these points abound. Hong Kong Telecommunications was awarded its licence to operate video on demand by Rita Lau, Hong Kong's deputy secretary for broadcasting, culture and sport, in late 1997.[5] Employees at Caterpillar, the world's largest manufacturer of construction and mining equipment, have been seeking to revoke, albeit unsuccessfully, Caterpillar's licence to operate since 1991. Founded in 1925, Caterpillar now employs just under 60,000 people and achieved record sales of $18.93 billion in 1997. Caterpillar products are manufactured in 38 different plants in the United States and a further 36 in the rest of the world. The global dealership network consists of 65 American and 132 non-American dealers, who serve customers in nearly 200 countries. Despite these accolades Caterpillar also has the somewhat dubious honour of being at the centre of one of the world's longest and most bitter industrial disputes. Workers at Caterpillar have not had a contract since 1991, when the company decided to break the union's insistence on industry-wide agreements, claiming it needed to be more flexible to compete successfully. Since then there have been two strikes, in 1991 and 1994. The second national stoppage lasted 17 months and the company managed to survive only by hiring temporary workers and because 4,000 Union of Auto Workers (UAW) members crossed the picket lines.[6]

Year 2000: the technological challenge

Numerous organisations risk losing their licences to operate at midnight on December 31st 1999, or before. As the bells toll and the new century is ushered in, computers the world over are predicted to malfunction. British Telecom has already declared that it cannot guarantee the phone lines will operate in 2000. Unilever has demanded that its suppliers demonstrate that they are 2000 compliant by the middle of 1999, threatening to terminate the contracts of any of those who are not. Midland Bank has predicted that one-fifth of companies will not survive. Frank Field, when minister for social services, declared: "If we [UK government] become aware that an organisation or supplier will not become Year 2000 compliant to our timetable ... we will review our contractual relationships with them, and consider alternative sources of supply." Mike Smith, a professor at St Bartholomew's Hospital in London, has predicted that the cost of the millennium bug for the National Health Service is likely to be £500m and that a 10% computer failure rate could result in up to 1,500 deaths.

Source: Taylor, I., "Guest column: This could be the Year of Panic", *Financial Times*, February 4th 1998.

Stakeholders as licensers

The variety of people who can affect whether or not an organisation retains its licence to operate is illustrated in the comments of Robert Berzok, who was responsible for employee communications at Union Carbide at the time of the Bhopal tragedy (see Chapter 7 for more details). He reports that in the wake of the disaster Union Carbide focused all its energies on keeping everyone affected by the disaster informed: the people of Bhopal; other communities in which the company did business, customers; shareholders; regulators; and legislators. Once these parties had been satisfied the business turned its attention internally, where morale had been shattered.

"Employees were faced with going to social gatherings, and on the one hand wanting to speak out about the company they worked for, which they knew was not the company being portrayed in the media, and on the other hand being embarrassed at being associated with this disaster".[7] As Berzok's comments suggest, the question of whether or not a given organisation is granted and subsequently retains its licence to operate is answered by those who are stakeholders in that organisation. The term stakeholder is much broader than that of shareholder, in that stakeholders include all those who interact with the organisation, whether they are external to it (customers and suppliers) or members of it (employees and owners – often the shareholders).

Customers as licensers
All organisations, whether manufacturing or service, profit or not-for-profit, public or private, have customers. Without them there would be no reason for the organisation to exist. This may be obvious, but it highlights the fact that customers are a powerful group of stakeholders in all organisations. Organisations exist to serve customers. Unless they are facing a monopoly, customers can choose where they take their business. In doing so, they decide to deal with certain organisations and not with others, thereby granting a licence to operate to the former and denying the latter. In extreme cases, where large numbers of customers decide to withdraw an organisation's licence to operate, the organisation can be forced to close, or at least exit the market concerned. Take, for example, Sony and its Betamax video technology. Although its product was widely seen as technically superior to the rival vhs technology, Sony failed to convince enough customers to grant it a licence to operate and was forced to make a humiliating and expensive withdrawal from the market and ultimately to license its competitor's vhs technology.

Suppliers as licensers
Organisations are increasingly outsourcing non-core activities and processes. Clive Thompson, chief executive of Rentokil, a UK-based services company, has built a highly successful business on the back of this trend. Rentokil started out as a pest exterminator, hence the name "Rent-to-Kill". Now Rentokil defines its market as looking after anything that takes place on other people's property and that they do not wish to look after themselves. Rentokil's sales grew at over 20% per year every year between 1982 and 1997. The business is now the world's largest supplier and maintainer of tropical plants. It offers cleaning services. It leases and maintains photocopiers. It provides security support. And it still exterminates vermin.

Support services, however, are not the only things being subcontracted. For many companies, particularly manufacturing companies, it is common for 40–50% of the finished product cost to be a result of bought-in items. The implication of this is that organisations, indeed entire supply chains, are becoming increasingly dependent upon one another. Although this offers advantages in terms of allowing organisations to focus their resources on their core areas of competence, it also increases their exposure, should a supplier deliberately or accidentally withdraw its support and hence an organisation's licence to operate. The 1995 Kobe earthquake is an example. During the earthquake one of Toyota's principal suppliers of springs was destroyed. A few days later Toyota was forced to close all its Japanese assembly plants while it hunted for an alternative supplier of springs.

Shareholders as licensers

Perhaps the most powerful group of licensers are the major institutional investors. Citywatch, a UK market research company, estimates that the top five fund managers own 26% of the FTSE 100, and that the top ten own 36%.[8] In the wake of the 1984 Bhopal disaster and a subsequent leak at another Union Carbide plant in West Virginia some eight months later, the company's shareholders began to withdraw their support for the business. Fuelled by rumours that the Indian government would seek millions of dollars in damages, the stock plummeted, reaching a sufficiently low level that GAF Corporation of New Jersey thought it worth launching a hostile takeover bid for Union Carbide. Union Carbide's response was to sell off many of its assets, buy back a massive 50% of its stock and in doing so, take on a $3.3 billion debt. Had these defensive actions not been successful, Union Carbide would undoubtedly have lost its licence to operate as an independent organisation and would have been subsumed into GAF Corporation.

Profit as a non-negotiable performance parameter

Many senior managers see profit as an essential measure of performance, yet for most organisations profit is merely one of the non-negotiable performance parameters and hence should not merit much discussion at the monthly board meeting.

Profit, as a measure of performance, reflects history. Today's profit is determined by decisions and actions that were taken yesterday. If today's profit is unacceptable short-term corrective actions can be taken, but to ensure the acceptability of tomorrow's profit, different dimensions of performance – the leading indicators, the determinants of tomorrow's performance – have to be considered.

This is why senior managers at organisations such as Nestlé have decided to stop reviewing profit at their monthly board meetings and instead rely on a continuous tracking system, which reports profit on a by-exception basis only.

Legislators as licensers

Licensers do not necessarily have to be intimately concerned with a single organisation. All organisations operate in markets, which are shaped by legal and political frameworks. Some, such as the Mafia, seek to ignore these, but the majority choose to operate within them, thereby accepting that legislators and politicians have the right to revoke the organisation's licence to operate should they feel it necessary to do so. An example of this is the UN's decision to impose sanctions on Iraq in the aftermath of the Gulf war. In doing so the UN revoked the licence to operate (in the world market) of many Iraqi businesses. Another example is the European Union's decision to ban the export of British beef, following the scare about Creutzfeldt-Jakob disease. In taking this decision the European Union was revoking the licence to operate, on the European stage, of British beef producers and exporters.

Regulators as licensers

In certain industries, especially those that have been recently privatised or are by nature monopolies (such as water, gas, power generation, telecommunications), official regulators have been appointed to ensure that organisations do not abuse the power granted to them when they are awarded licences to operate. Regulators often define specific performance standards and expectations, and they have the authority to penalise organisations that fail to live up to these standards. Sometimes they revoke the licence to operate of established players and then grant these vacant licences to aspiring new players. The UK water industry, regulated by Office of Water Services (OFWAT), is an example. Every year all water and sewerage companies in England and Wales have to submit to OFWAT detailed statistics on their service delivery performance. The topics covered include inadequate pressure, supply interruptions, restrictions on water use, flooding from sewers, billing contacts, written complaints, bills for metered customers and ease of telephone contact. OFWAT releases an annual level of service report, which allows customers to compare the levels of service offered by different firms and identifies benchmark levels of service based on the performance of firms in other regulated industries, such as electricity, gas and telecommunications. The importance of these comparative data is illustrated by the fact that Ian Byatt, director-general of OFWAT, has declared that he is planning to use them to reward companies which have delivered above-average service and penalise those which have delivered below-average service in the 1999 price review.[9]

The licence to operate of individuals
Individuals within organisations are also granted licences to operate, which in some cases are official. Professionals such as chartered engineers, certified accountants and lawyers are granted licences by their associations. In other cases licences are unofficial, in the sense that they are not externally verified, but they are still licences. An example is an individual's contract of employment. This licence to operate is granted to the individual by the organisation in recognition of the fact that the individual is a member of the organisation and has the right to act on its behalf. Of course, licences such as contracts of employment can be revoked at any time. Gross misconduct, failure to perform, failure to adhere to organisational rules and expectations can all lead to dismissal, which in effect involves revoking the individual's licence.

Identifying the non-negotiable performance parameters
Identifying which performance parameters are non-negotiable for a given organisation is a challenging task made simpler by the checksheet shown in Figure 4.1. The process involves asking three critical questions:

1 Which dimensions of performance do the stakeholders see as non-negotiable?
2 What level of performance does the organisation have to achieve with regard to each of these non-negotiable performance parameters?
3 How can the organisation be sure to achieve the required levels of performance?

The critical questions

4.1

	Which dimensions of performance do the stakeholders see as non-negotiable?	What level of performance does the organisation have to achieve with regard to each of these non-negotiable performance parameters?	How can the organisation be sure to achieve the required levels of performance?
Customers as licensers			
Suppliers as licensers			
Shareholders as licensers			
Employees as licensers			
Legislators as licensers			
Regulators as licensers			

Losing a licence to operate

The common theme underlying the preceding discussion is that organisations and individuals lose their licences to operate when the people who awarded them withdraw support. Politicians fail to get re-elected when voters lose confidence in them; airlines or bus operators would have their licences to operate revoked, by either the general public or the relevant authority, if too many of their planes or buses crashed; and so on. The reason an organisation or individual loses its licence to operate is because it fails to meet expectations against some critical performance parameter. The only people who can define these parameters are the stakeholders, for they are the ones who decide when to withdraw support. For hospitals the critical performance parameters might include hygiene, quality of diagnosis and quality of treatment. For the managing director of a manufacturing business the non-negotiable parameters might include business profitability and shareholder returns. For a charity they might include image and reputation in the eyes of donors. The point is that for all organisations there are parameters which are so critical that failure to control performance against any of them can have serious, and sometimes immediate consequences for the business.

Measures as a means of ensuring compliance

How can organisations ensure that they never fail to deliver against their non-negotiable parameters? At one level this question can be answered by looking at the fail-safe precautions, and in extreme cases contingency plans, that organisations adopt. Hospitals have emergency generators so that if their main power supply fails they can continue to operate. Planes usually have more than one engine, despite the fact that the power generated by a single engine is sufficient to fly with. But fail-safe precautions are not always practical, often because of the cost involved. It is in such circumstances that measures can be used as a means of ensuring compliance. Three basic strategies can be adopted: preventative control; pre-emptive control; and predictive control.

Preventative systems

The classic preventative measurement systems are audits and inspections. These can be conducted by either internal or external parties. Generally, they seek to establish whether the procedures being followed by members of the organisation and the working practices that have been adopted are likely to result in performance failures. Such inspections take place at regular intervals in most organisations and are also specially commissioned, in the form of inquiries, when major performance failures occur.

Nortel's environmental management system

Nortel, a telecommunications operator, with annual sales of $15.45 billion in 1997 and 73,000 employees worldwide, operates an environmental management system in each of its global locations.[10] The corporate environmental management system standard sets global corporate expectations, but each location is required to implement its own environmental management system, which will allow it to monitor its own environmental impact and establish the procedures and systems that suit local conditions. Each location also sets its own goals, which are aligned to or exceed the overall corporate objectives. Every two years each location is audited against requirements of the standard. For Nortel an environmental effect is defined as "any change to the environment, whether adverse or beneficial, wholly or partially resulting from activities, products or services of the organisation". Nortel's corporate policy requires that each of its locations shall:

- comply with all relevant legislation and with the specific requirements to which it has made a public commitment;
- reinforce the environmental management system standard and principles it represents;
- commit to adherence to all corporate environmental standards and programmes, including objectives and targets;
- adhere to the principle of continual improvement;
- communicate and report progress over time to all employees and groups within the organisation.

The standard requires that each location adopts the relevant corporate procedure for identifying the environmental effects of its activities, products and services and uses this procedure to classify the effects as "controllable", "influenceable" or "unclassified". Controllable effects are defined as "all significant effects that Northern Telecom could directly control if it so chose", for example: emissions to atmosphere; discharges to water; solid waste generation; land or ground water contamination; consumption of energy and natural resources; and noise and odour. Influenceable effects are defined as "those significant effects from the goods and services acquired or used by Northern Telecom which are beyond direct Northern Telecom control". Examples include mercury in components, and toxic elements in products and packaging materials. Unclassified effects are defined as "those effects, which are currently considered as neither controllable nor influenceable, but which can be said to have an undesirable effect on the environment".

The measurement system which surrounds this programme and allows Nortel to check whether specific locations have established appropriate procedures, and hence minimised the likelihood that they will infringe any of its non-negotiable environmental performance parameters, is described in the corporate standard. This states: "Nortel's senior management have the responsibility of identifying an individual or a specific function who shall be responsible, irrespective of other duties, for: ensuring the requirements of this standard are met; and reporting on the organisation's performance in the implementation of this standard."

The same standard also states that each unit's EMS should be audited on a regular basis to establish whether the EMS in operation:

▰ conforms to the standard and is properly implemented and maintained;
▰ is effective in meeting policies and procedures;
▰ is effective in meeting objectives and targets.

ICL policy framework and audit

ICL, a computer services company employing some 19,000 people worldwide and 84% owned by Japanese multinational Fujitsu, operates a global policy compliance audit. In the introduction to the document describing the policy framework, Keith Todd, ICL's chief executive, states: "Although I would like everyone to have as much freedom of operation as possible there are some rules which have to be followed in all organisations, and you need to know what they are to operate with confidence." Estelle Clark, director of quality, continues by explaining that the ICL policy framework brings together, in one document, all the company's mandatory policies, and points out that there are three main reasons for policies to be declared mandatory:

▰ Because of legislative requirements (because by doing so business risk will be minimised), or because they reflect good business practice.

◪ Because they underpin ICL's group strategies, or because they help
  support the ICL brand.
◪ Because they reinforce ICL's values.

ICL's policy framework is wide-ranging and covers issues such as human
resources, sales, quality and customer care, product conformity, finance and
business planning, inter-business trading, corporate security, commercial
and legal, export control, data protection, year 2000, information systems
and IT security, external communications, internal communications and
environment. The main body of the document lists all the mandatory
policies and then provides a series of critical questions, which ICL executives
use to audit their own business units on an annual basis. Under the section
describing the quality and customer care policies, for example, the manual
states that all businesses will do the following:

◪ Implement policy deployment and the BREAKTHROUGH initiative.
◪ Apply the Product Life Cycle Management process to all product
  developments.
◪ Apply the Service Policies set by the Service Strategy Board, including
  the Service Life Cycle Management process, to all services.
◪ Apply the Project Delivery Framework to all projects.
◪ Use the Customer Satisfaction Measurement Framework.
◪ Register their quality management system to ISO 9000.
◪ Use self-assessment and the Business Excellence Model as their
  framework for Business Development.
◪ Operate the Excellence Awards Process, or equivalent recognition
  scheme, to recognise staff achievement and role model behaviour.
◪ Apply a local customer complaints/customer satisfaction process to
  resolve all customer issues which results in early escalation of severe
  customer dissatisfaction to the Customer Red Alert Process.

The ten audit questions that relate to these policies follow on the next
page of the manual:

◪ Are up-to-date copies of *Quality and Customer Care Policy and Practice*,
  The Project Delivery Framework, *Managing the Product Life Cycle*,
  Services Policies, *Managing the Service Life Cycle* and the *Customer
  Satisfaction Measurement Framework* readily available to all staff who
  have a need for them?
◪ Do you have a way of ensuring that the Product Life Cycle Management

process is applied to all product developments?

- ◪ Do you have a way of ensuring that the Services Policies, including the Service Life Cycle Management Process, are applied to all services?
- ◪ Do you have a way of ensuring that the Project Delivery Framework is applied to all projects?
- ◪ Do you operate a customer satisfaction measurement programme that covers levels 1, 2 and 3 of the Customer Satisfaction Measurement Framework?
- ◪ Is your Quality Management System registered to ISO 9000 with a way of ensuring that you retain your registered status?
- ◪ Do you have a self-assessment process in place which helps identify and monitors the successful completion of priority actions identified in your strategic plan?
- ◪ Do you operate the Excellence Awards process such that anyone in your business can receive appropriate recognition for outstanding achievement and role model behaviour?
- ◪ Do you operate a process which results in a timely response to all customer complaints?
- ◪ Do you operate an escalation process which results in the early escalation of severe customer dissatisfaction through your local process to a Customer Red Alert?

The Nortel and ICL cases illustrate how audits can be used by management to ensure that the necessary systems and procedures are in place to reduce the chances that an organisation will fail to deliver on any of its non-negotiable performance parameters. The weakness of such preventative approaches, however, is that they are often infrequent. In the case of Nortel, audits of the environmental management system take place every two years. The implication is that a given Nortel business may have been operating an inappropriate procedure for up to two years before it is discovered. In some cases this would undoubtedly be unacceptable and hence the use of more frequent control-based measurement systems or pre-emptive systems would be more appropriate.

Pre-emptive systems

Pre-emptive measurement control systems differ from preventative systems in that they involve continuous scanning. Preventative measurement control systems are designed to audit whether or not the correct systems and procedures are in place. Pre-emptive measurement control systems are designed to monitor continually whether the organisation has infringed one or more of its non-negotiable performance parameters.

Jacques Horovitz, one of the first people to study the strategic control systems used by organisations, provides an example of such a system. In his paper Horovitz describes the pre-emptive control systems adopted by an electronics company, which had chosen to compete on the basis of customer satisfaction.[11] The industry was strongly driven by equipment reliability, and with this in mind the company had declared to all of its customers "no piece of equipment sold to our customers will ever be down for more than 12 hours". Partly to reinforce the importance of this message and partly to enable senior managers to monitor whether this non-negotiable performance parameter was ever infringed, the company instituted a system whereby the chief executive was told every morning and every afternoon if a piece of the company's equipment had been down for more than 12 hours. To ensure that this happened a simple, systematic procedure was established. If any service agent was unable to repair any piece of equipment within two hours he was required to inform his supervisor. If a further two hours elapsed and the equipment had still not been repaired, the supervisor was required to inform his supervisor, and so on up the chain until the message reached the chief executive. The beauty of this process lay in its simplicity and in the fact that the chief executive was made aware immediately if the organisation was in danger of infringing one of its own non-negotiable performance parameters, and hence could take personal corrective action to rectify the situation.

Predictive systems

In an ideal world the non-negotiable performance parameters would never be infringed and all organisations would have early-warning systems in place to advise them that a non-negotiable parameter was about to be infringed. It is unlikely that any organisation will be able to cover all eventualities in this way, simply because some infringements may be unforeseeable. There are, however, techniques in the quality management area that could be used to establish early-warning systems for certain processes.

One of the best examples is statistical process control. Techniques such as control charts are well established within manufacturing environments, where it is accepted they can provide an early warning that a manufacturing process is going out of control. What appears to have been forgotten, however, is the history of these techniques, which suggests that they can be applied to wider business problems. W. Edwards Deming, widely recognised as the father of statistical quality control, first applied his ideas when working on the US census in the late 1930s and early 1940s. He concentrated on routine clerical operations, such as coding and card punching. By bringing these processes under statistical control, and then concentrating on process redesign, he was able to reduce the need for inspection and verification enormously. The associated cost savings were significant and amounted to several hundreds of thousands of dollars (at 1940 prices).[12]

If Deming could apply his statistical techniques to non-manufacturing operations in the 1930s and 1940s, why can organisations not do the same today? For if they could, and if they applied them to the right processes (that is, those whose failure to deliver could lead to non-negotiable performance parameters being infringed), they would have truly predictive measurement control systems capable of providing early warnings that if no corrective action is taken the organisation will infringe one of its non-negotiable performance parameters.

Control charts: a solution?

Control charts are a well-established method of controlling the quality of output of manufacturing processes. They are based on the premise that the output of any process will vary. Imagine, for example, a McDonald's restaurant. Despite the fact that all McDonald's restaurants follow the same basic procedure when making a hamburger and use the same basic ingredients, no two hamburgers produced by any McDonald's restaurant will be identical. One will be slightly larger than the other, or slightly rounder, or slightly hotter, or slight flatter. The output of any process will vary across a whole host of dimensions, of which some will be critical to customers and others will be less important. The theory behind statistical process control (SPC) is that each of these dimensions will vary according to a normal distribution, the classic bell-shaped curve.

The statistical theory associated with the normal distribution is well developed and widely understood. Quality experts have used this theory to design a series of charts, known as process control charts, which can be used to track whether or not processes are "in control", that is, whether or not the outputs being produced by the process conform with the outputs that would be expected according to statistical theory. The method used to track whether or not a process is in control is simple. The outputs produced by the process are sampled at regular intervals and the data gathered are plotted on an appropriate control chart. All control charts incorporate upper and lower action and warning limits. By convention, the warning limits are set at a level such that the probability of any observation falling outside either warning limit is 1 in 40. Similarly, the action limits are set so that the probability of any observation falling outside either action limit is 1 in 1,000. Standard rules of thumb are then used to assess whether the process being monitored is going out of control. Typical rules include:

- any single sample falling outside the upper or the lower action limits;
- any two consecutive samples falling outside either warning limit;
- any run of six consecutive samples in the same direction.

Although there are some technical difficulties, control charts could be designed such that if the rules of thumb suggested that the process was going out of control, this would indicate that one of the organisation's non-negotiable performance parameters was in danger of being infringed.

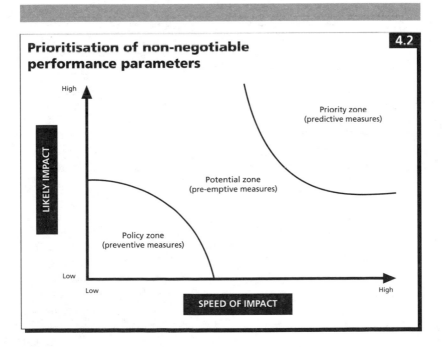

Prioritisation of non-negotiable performance parameters

4.2

Priority zone
(predictive measures)

Potential zone
(pre-emptive measures)

Policy zone
(preventive measures)

LIKELY IMPACT

High

Low

SPEED OF IMPACT

Low

High

Putting the theory into practice

Developing measurement systems which ensure an organisation does not breach any of its non-negotiable performance parameters involves two main steps. First, as already discussed, it is necessary to identify which performance parameters are seen as non-negotiable by the organisation's stakeholders (see Figure 4.1 on page 99 for a simple way of doing this). Second, it is necessary to prioritise these non-negotiable parameters by looking at the likely impact infringements will have on the business and how rapidly the impact will be felt (see Figure 4.2 on the previous page).

For those non-negotiable parameters that fall within the priority zone (that is, high and rapid impact), it is essential that, if possible, predictive measurement systems are found and implemented. For those that fall in the potential zone, pre-emptive measurement systems are acceptable if preventative ones cannot be found. For those non-negotiable performance parameters with low and slow impact (that is, those that fall into the policy zone), preventative measurement systems, such as ICL's policy framework and audit, are often adequate.

5 Checking health

OVER the years the medical profession has been able to develop robust processes for checking the health of individuals. General practitioners (GPs) have a battery of standard tests that they run when people come for a check-up. Blood pressure, heart rates, cholesterol levels, weight and ease of breathing are reviewed and compared with expected norms. Qualitative data, such as how patients look and whether they appear unduly tired, are also gathered. On the basis of these data the GP makes an assessment of the health of the individual. Corrective action plans, such as "you should try to reduce your cholesterol intake", may be recommended. In some cases further, more detailed tests will be arranged. Thus the medical profession has at its disposal a hierarchical battery of diagnostic tests that it can use to identify any potential threats to the long-term viability of individuals, and to pinpoint the root causes of these threats. The question this chapter seeks to address is: how can the same set of diagnostic tests be established for an organisation?

The chapter consists of four main sections. The first two review the diagnostic tests various organisations have used to assess their health as well as covering financial health and customer satisfaction. There are several business performance frameworks that can be used to assess an organisation's health. The most notable are the Deming Prize, the Baldridge Award, the European Foundation for Quality Management Award and the Balanced Business Scorecard. The third section of this chapter reviews these and other frameworks, commenting on their strengths and weaknesses. The last section draws these themes together by explaining how a hierarchical battery of tests can be used to check the health of an organisation.

Checking financial health

"Cash is a necessary condition. When you have enough, cash does not matter. When you don't have enough, nothing else matters."[1] The fundamental measure of the financial health of any business is cash. Cash is real. Cash is tangible. Profit, return on investment and operating expenses are all figments of the established accounting systems. Cash is not. It is something you either have, or you do not have.

Bankruptcy in the United States

The number of businesses filing for bankruptcy in the United States peaked in 1987, when 82,446 firms were declared bankrupt. By 1997 the equivalent figure was 54,027. Research conducted by Professor Roy Warner on behalf of the American Bankruptcy Institute identified the most common causes of bankruptcy as mismanagement (mentioned by 82% of respondents) and market forces (mentioned by 68% of respondents). Of course, both mismanagement and market forces can result in cashflow crises, which means that the bills cannot be paid and hence bankruptcy beckons.

Source: Web site http://www.abiworld.org.

Cash, however, is only one of several measures used by managers to check the financial health of their businesses. For although cash is a useful indication of whether or not an organisation is likely to survive, it is of limited relevance when it comes to making investment decisions. It is widely accepted that one of the first organisations to face this problem was the DuPont Powder Company. Around 1900 the three DuPont cousins acquired the assets of E.I. DuPont de Nemours Powder Company. They started a process of vertical integration through which they created one of the first multidivisional companies. To manage such a company it was essential to develop a centralised accounting system, not least because this would enable senior managers to:

- control, co-ordinate and assess the horizontal flow of operations among the company's three main departments – manufacturing, sales and purchasing;
- plan the company's long-range development.

Central to the role of long-range development is the question of capital allocation. Before the advent of centralised accounting systems, managers had no objective means of assessing the performance of different business units and hence deciding to whom they should allocate their limited budget. To solve this problem DuPont, under the guidance of Donaldson Brown, the chief executive, developed and introduced the pyramid of financial ratios shown in Figure 5.1.[2]

DuPont's pyramid of financial ratios

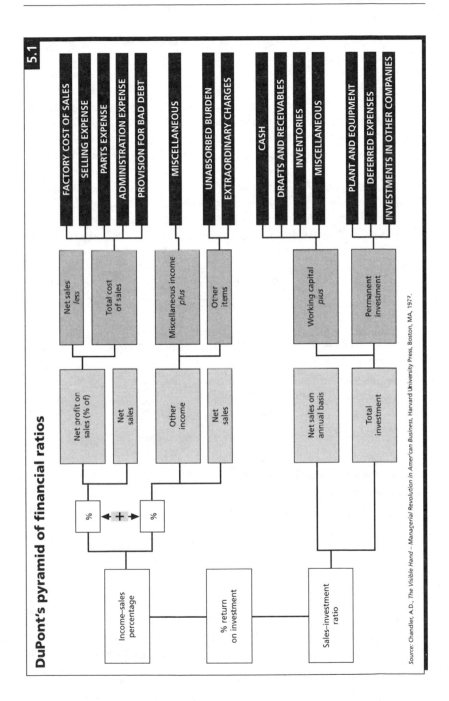

5.1

Source: Chandler, A.D., *The Visible Hand – Managerial Revolution in American Business*, Harvard University Press, Boston, MA, 1977.

The fact that most organisations operate similar, if not identical, pyramids of financial ratios today illustrates the appeal and durability of this approach. BTR, a British conglomerate, operates a sophisticated and coherently structured profit planning process. The basis of BTR's process is that profit improvement should come from three sources: increased sales volume; increased productivity; and improved margins. Sir Owen Green, who stepped down as chairman in 1993, introduced this philosophy of continuous cost reduction and margin enhancement to BTR. During the 1960s, 1970s and 1980s BTR grew as a result of an aggressive acquisitions policy. Companies taken over included Leyland, Birmingham Rubber Co, Thomas Tilling and Dunlop Holdings in the UK, Berg-Warner Australia, and ACI International and Stewart-Warner in the United States. By 1993 the company had nearly 1,500 subsidiaries in 60 countries. Unlike many other industrial conglomerates, however, BTR's strategy was to develop the capabilities of the manufacturing companies it took over, rather than milk them. Hence expenditure of $800m per year on manufacturing equipment for the five years ending 1993.[3]

Profit planning at BTR

All managing directors of business units within BTR are expected to compete, submit and defend their profit plans for the next 12 months on an annual basis. In simple terms the profit plan consists of a series of schedules (PP1–PP9).

- PP1 Results and ratios
- PP2 Profit before interest and tax
- PP3 Sales change
- PP3A Material cost-of-sales change
- PP3B Sales and cost-of-sales change
- PP4 Payroll
- PP4A Payroll detail
- PP5 Overheads
- PP6 Profit change summary
- PP7 Capital expenditure
- PP8 Balance sheet
- PP8A Working capital
- PP9 Cashflow

Of these, the critical schedule is PP6, which summarises the impact of all the other schedules. PP6 analyses profit change compared with the previous year and establishes the extent to which changes are a function of:

∎ inflation and price, either sales or materials, changes;
∎ productivity gains and development costs;
∎ volume and mix changes.

The unwritten rules in BTR are that businesses should not seek to grow their profits too rapidly (1–2% annual growth is adequate), and that profit improvements should come in roughly equal amounts from price changes, productivity gains and volume and mix changes. The explicit nature of the profit plan (and the accompanying schedules) makes it easy to identify:

∎ whether these rules are being adhered to;
∎ whether the profit plan that has been proposed is considered and attainable;
∎ whether the managers proposing the plan are seeking to sacrifice the long-term health of the business for short-term gain.

Senior managers at BTR attribute much of the company's success to the profit planning process. Indeed, several have gone as far as suggesting that one of the reasons for BTR's recent difficulties is that the profit planning process has been made too complex and is now being used as a stick with which to beat management, rather than a structured and transparent method of planning moderate profit growth, thereby ensuring long-term business success.

Modern methods of checking financial health

Accounting historians, such as Geoffrey Chandler and H. Thomas Johnson, report that most of the cost accounting concepts in use today (such as overhead allocation, fixed and variable costing) had been developed by the 1920s. Most of these concepts remained largely unchallenged until the 1980s. Since then various alternative techniques and frameworks have been proposed, most notably activity-based costing (ABC), throughput accounting and shareholder value analysis – market value added (MVA™) and economic value added (EVA™).[4] The first two have been suggested as better methods for valuing products, and the third and fourth are more concerned with valuing businesses.

Product costing: Activity Based Costing...
Activity based costing and throughput accounting are founded on the concern that traditional methods of product costing are fundamentally flawed. The basis of this concern is that standard methods of accounting which allocate overhead in proportion to the amount of direct labour required to make a product are no longer valid. Increasing automation has meant that the proportion of finished product cost attributable to direct labour can now be as low as 5–10%, whereas that attributable to overhead can be as high as 50%. Thus allocating overhead on the basis of labour can result in wildly erroneous product costs and a gross misunderstanding of the organisation's cost base. Activity based costing and throughput accounting take account of these concerns by focusing on activities and seeking to identify where in the manufacturing process cost is really incurred.

The fundamental concept in activity based costing is that of the cost driver. This allows costs to be traced from activities to products, based on the product's demand for these activities during the production process. Typical cost drivers include set-up times, number of components, frequency of product order and frequency of product shipment. In a traditional costing system, where overhead is allocated on the basis of direct labour, two products which require the same amount of direct labour input will attract the same proportion of overhead, even if one requires a machine set-up that takes three days and the other requires a machine set-up that takes three minutes. Similarly, if one product consists of 20 components, which have to be ordered from 20 different suppliers, and the other consists of two components, both of which can be ordered from the same supplier, because both products require the same direct labour input both will attract an equal proportion of the overhead incurred through the purchasing process. Advocates of activity based costing argue that this is clearly unfair and suggest that baskets of cost drivers are identified and that overhead is allocated in line with these real cost drivers, rather than on the basis of the proxy (and highly inaccurate) cost driver, direct labour content.[5]

...and throughput accounting
Throughput accounting adopts a radically different basis for the determination of cost and concentrates on the bottleneck or capacity-

constrained resource. Advocates of throughput accounting base their arguments on Eli Goldratt's belief that the critical resource in any manufacturing facility is the capacity-constrained resource or bottleneck.[7] In Goldratt's view a bottleneck constrains the output of a manufacturing system and hence an hour lost at the bottleneck is an hour lost for the system as a whole. Imagine, for example, a production process with three stages. The first machine can produce at a rate of 250 units per hour, the second at a rate of 450 units per hour and the third at a rate of 20 units per hour. If all units have to be processed by all three machines, then the maximum output from this process would be 20 units per hour, as this is the rate at which the bottleneck (the third machine) can process products. The implication is that an hour lost at either of the first two machines is unimportant; it costs the organisation nothing in terms of lost output. An hour lost at the third machine, however, costs the organisation the market value of 20 units, assuming that everything produced can be sold. This is because an hour lost at a bottleneck can never be replaced as the bottleneck, by definition, is fully utilised and therefore has no spare production capacity.

Applying this argument to product costing, the critical issue becomes not how much direct labour input the product requires, but how much of the bottleneck's time the product requires. Consider, for example, two products which have the same overall direct labour content. Product A takes twice as much time at the bottleneck machine so it can be manufactured only half as fast as product B. Thus for every two units of product B only one unit of product A can be manufactured. Traditional cost accounting would attribute the same level of overhead to both these products, yet product B costs the organisation far less to produce than product A as it does not require as much time at the bottleneck machine. Advocates of throughput accounting argue that unless organisations consider this when pricing products, they are deluding themselves about the margins they are actually generating, and, more importantly, not realising the margins they could be generating.[7]

Critics of these two methods of costing highlight their complexity to implement and question whether the product costs that result are any more valid than those generated by traditional methods of cost accounting. There are difficulties in identifying and assigning cost to the real cost drivers, and bottlenecks are rarely static in manufacturing firms, shifting as the product and volume mix changes. Nevertheless, both methods are widely accepted as alternative ways of product costing which can be used in parallel with more traditional approaches to provide additional insight into the financial health of the business.

Valuing businesses – shareholder value[9]

One challenge that faces both managers and investors is how to assess whether the business is generating value or wealth. The problem with traditional measures of wealth generation, especially profit, is that they ignore the cost of capital. A business can show an accounting profit but still fail to deliver a true economic profit, because the rate at which it is generating a return is lower than the rate at which investors could generate a return by investing in other securities of comparable risk. Most of the major consultancies now offer value-based measurement systems designed to overcome this problem. Stern Stewart, a New York-based consultancy, is the leader in the field. So popular are its ideas of economic value analysis (EVA™) and market value analysis (MVA™) that the firm has now trademarked them. Put simply, EVA™ is the net operating profit after tax minus an appropriate charge for the opportunity cost of all capital invested in the business (see below). Stern Stewart's argument is that EVA™ provides a more valid measure of profit precisely because it takes account of the cost of capital and therefore encourages managers to think constantly about whether they are destroying or creating value for the owners of the business. The strength of EVA™ is its apparent simplicity. It has been likened to a measure of total factor productivity for an enterprise and, as with most measures of productivity, immediately highlights several ways in which performance can be improved:

- Earn more profit without using more capital.
- Use less capital or lower the cost of capital.
- Increase investment in projects that generate rates of return greater than their costs of capital.
- Curtail investments in projects that generate rates of return less than their costs of capital.

Getting to EVA™

Calculating the EVA™ of an organisation is a simple process, although Stern Stewart claims that up to 173 minor adjustments have to be made to the final value to ensure its validity. Ignoring these, however, the calculation of EVA™ involves three steps:

- the amount of capital tied up in the business has to be established;

- ☑ the cost of this capital has to be determined;
- ☑ these two figures are multiplied together and subtracted from the organisation's operating earnings (less tax).

If the resultant value is positive the organisation is generating wealth; if it is negative the organisation is destroying it.

Calculating the amount of capital

For exponents of EVA™ the capital tied up in an operation consists of the costs of all the assets plus working capital plus other long-term investments. Although traditional accounting rules suggest that expenditure on employee training and R&D are period expenses, they are in fact long-term investments. Hence they should be included in the calculation to determine the total amount of capital tied up in the business.

Calculating the cost of capital

The cost of borrowed capital is easy to establish, for in the short term it is the interest paid adjusted to reflect tax deductions. Such an approach, however, misses the cost of equity capital – the money shareholders provide. Often managers assume this money is free, but it is not. At least not as far as the shareholders are concerned, for they view the cost of their capital as the return they could be making if they invested their money in another portfolio of similar risk. In today's markets equity costs hover at around 12% (6% because this is the rate at which stocks have grown on average over the years and a further 6% because this is the average dividend that shareholders receive). The actual cost of capital for a business is therefore the weighted average of its borrowed capital and its equity capital.

Source: Tully, S., "The Real Key to Creating Wealth", http://www.sternstewart.com.

MVA™ is closely related to EVA™, with the distinction that MVA™ considers the difference between the market value of an enterprise and the economic value of the capital it employs (see Table 5.1 on the next page for an analysis of MVA™ in the United States). Business interest in both of these measures is growing rapidly. Roberto Goizueta, former chief executive of Coca-Cola, for example, is on record as saying: "It [EVA™] is the way to keep score. Why everybody doesn't use it is a mystery to me."[9]

Table 5.1 **Top ten American firms by MVA**

| Company | 1996 | | 1991 | 1995 | 1996 |
	MVA	Market value	MVA rank	MVA rank	MVA rank
Coca-Cola	124,894	135,708	4	1	1
General Electric	121,874	175,441	6	2	2
Microsoft	89,957	95,638	14	5	3
Intel	86,481	103,964	74	12	4
Merck	78,246	100,466	2	3	5
Philip Morris	66,608	109,493	3	4	6
Exxon	55,532	143,928	12	9	7
Procter & Gamble	55,102	80,134	10	8	8
Bristol-Myers Squibb	51,119	69,257	7	6	9
Pfizer	42,910	57,017	5	11	10

Source: Stern Stewart web site (http://www.sternstewart.com/perf_rankings/frameset).

Michael Riley, chief financial officer of the United States Postal Service, was featured in the November 1995 issue of *CFO Magazine* saying: "EVA™ brings together all aspects of the business into one measure. It changes the focus from the traditional government culture. We will learn to grow revenue only when it is profitable, to invest more only when it produces a good return, and to reduce expenses only when it doesn't hurt service."

Randall Tobias, chairman and chief executive of Eli Lilley, responding to the question "Why did you link compensation to EVA™?" is reported to have said:

"We had a cross-functional team, which for some time had been examining what we saw as a shortcoming of our incentive system – that executive pay was linked to sales and net income. There just wasn't a very good correlation at all with shareholder value. So with EVA™ consultant Stern Stewart we developed a pay plan that fitted our needs.

Basically, Lilley's bonus plan now requires managers to achieve continuous, year-to-year improvements in EVA™. First we set EVA™ targets based on competitive factors. As a hypothetical example, let's say we have a 10% cost of capital, and each year the bar is raised. It's a small percentage increase, but it keeps pounding at you. Whatever you did yesterday, you need to do better tomorrow to keep raising shareholder value. If the targets are met or exceeded, there's a bonus, based on a proprietary formula. Last year, for example, the company did very well. Many managers got bonuses worth close to 50% of their total compensation.

The bottom line is that as you're making decisions you've got to think about aligning them with EVA™. It's easy to see EVA™ as a very sophisticated financial tool, and indeed it is, but I think it's important to understand that it is really a tool to change behaviour too. Linking bonuses to EVA™ is meant to change the whole culture."[10]

EVA™ at Varity

Victor Rice, chairman and chief executive of New York-based automotive components and diesel engine manufacturer Varity, decided to adopt EVA™ as a company-wide performance indicator in 1993. He reports that in 1992 Varity's "EVA™ was minus $150m". In other words, the company's cost of capital exceeded its operating profit by $150m at that time. EVA™ enabled Varity's management to take a close look at the organisation's capital structure and to recognise that, relatively speaking, equity cost more than debt. Since then Varity's EVA™ models have been used to confirm decisions to build new facilities, such as the anti-lock brake system manufacturing facilities in Flowerville, MI, and Heerlen, Netherlands, and to evaluate potential joint ventures, such as the one between UK-based Perkins and Ishikawajima-Shibaura Machinery Company of Japan.

EVA™ permeates the whole of Varity. It features in the company's vision statement: "Our goal is to maximise the total cash return to our shareholders over the long term." It is used in the strategic planning process to quantify the potential impact of proposed initiatives, such as expanding into a new market. It is even used to evaluate the impact of quality improvement teams, as they seek to reduce cycle times and hence decrease the amount of capital tied up in inventories.

At Varity Perkins the notion of EVA™ has been adopted so completely that all 4,000 employees participate in an EVA™-based compensation plan – if EVA™ in their business unit increases so does their compensation. As far as Rice is concerned this is perfect, for in his view employees have to think like shareholders when they are asked to manage EVA™.

Source: Stern Stewart web site (http://sternstewart.com).

It is not only managers, however, who believe in the power of value generation measures. Increasingly, Wall Street and the City of London are turning to these measures to evaluate business performance. Eugene Vesell, senior vice-president of Oppenheimer Capital, which manages $26 billion and has earned an average of 17% annually for the past decade, says: "We like to invest in companies that use EVA™ and similar measures. Making higher returns than the cost of capital is how we look at the world."[11]

Ian Rennardson, a conglomerates analyst at Merrill Lynch, is reported to have said: "These types of measurement give you a fantastic handle on where companies have gone right and wrong historically, particularly for companies that have made a lot of acquisitions. A lot of people in the City are now using them".[12]

Perhaps even more telling are the results of research conducted by Professors Lehn and Makihja of the University of Pittsburgh. They followed the performance of 241 companies over the period 1987–93, tracking the relationship between EVA™ and MVA™ and stock performance. They found that both EVA™ and MVA™ were significantly positively correlated with stock performance and that chief executive officer (CEO) turnover was negatively correlated with these two measures. In other words, companies with poor EVA™ or MVA™ were more likely to change or fire their CEOs. Although not particularly surprising, this latter finding provides yet another spur to CEOs who are considering whether to adopt value generation-based measures to assess the health of their businesses.

Checking health: the customer's view

Traditionally, businesses have measured customer satisfaction reactively by counting the number of complaints received. Research, however, has shown that this approach is fundamentally flawed because few customers complain. Most just defect and advise their friends to do the same. As discussed in Chapter 1, increasing recognition of this, and of the fact that satisfied customers are not necessarily loyal customers, has resulted in businesses adopting ever more sophisticated methods of tracking customer satisfaction. Gone are the days of waiting for customers to complain. Now is the era of customer satisfaction surveys, mystery shopping and focus groups (see later).

Customer complaints and defections: the research evidence

Technical Assistance Research Programmes (TARP), a US-based market research organisation, has been exploring customer satisfaction and defections since the mid-1980s. Its research suggests that only 20% of dissatisfied customers actually complain and as few as 4% go to the trouble of writing. Of those who do complain, only 5% address their complaints to senior management, with 45% of them relying on frontline staff to solve the problem. In terms of impact, TARP's research suggests that:

◪ 85% of customers who experience no problem with the product or service will repeat their purchase;
◪ only 45% of those who are dissatisfied and who complain will repurchase;
◪ where the complainant is mollified the repurchase percentage rises to around 80%;
◪ where the complainant is satisfied the repeat purchase percentage exceeds 90% (ie, people who complain and are satisfied with the way the company handles their complaint are more likely to repeat their purchase than people who never experienced a problem in the first place).

Source: Technical Assistance Research Programs, *Consumer Complaint Handling in America: An Update Study*, US Office of Consumer Affairs, March 1986.

Customer satisfaction surveys

Numerous organisations use questionnaires to gather data on customer satisfaction. Their advantage is that they allow a lot of data to be captured quickly and cheaply. In theory, their disadvantage is that they rarely provide qualitative insights. In practice, the most significant weakness of the customer satisfaction questionnaires used by most organisations is that their design is appalling. Take, for example, the questionnaire shown in Figure 5.2 on the next page, which is an exact copy of one used by a five-star South American hotel.

There are numerous problems with this questionnaire.

◪ There is no explanation of the scale to be used. Respondents are

Sample customer satisfaction questionnaire 5.2

Hotel
La Fontana

CALIDAD DEL SERVICIO

Gracias por sus comentarios
Thank you for your comments

№ - 411

FECHA: _____
Date

NOMBRE: _____   COMPAÑIA: _____
Name   Company

DIRECCION: _____   HABITACION No.: _____
Address   Room No.

POR QUE ESCOGIO NUESTRO HOTEL   WHY DID YOU CHOOSE OUR HOTEL

Vió un aviso publicitario   ☐   You saw an advertisement

Su compañía lo recomendó   ☐   Your company recommended it

Recibió información del Hotel directamente ☐ You were informed directly by the Hotel

Otros: _____   Others: _____

CALIFIQUE EL SERVICIO DE 1 A 10
(Qualify service from 1 to 10)

ALOJAMIENTO (Lodgment)

1. SERVICIO DE RECEPCION ___   6. SERVICIO DE BOTONES ___
   Reception service   Bell boys service

2. PRESENTACION DE LA HABITACION ___ 7. COMUNICACION TELEFONICA ___
   Room commodity   Telephone system service

3. SERVICIO EN EL GIMNASIO ___   8. SERVICIO DE MENSAJES ___
   Fitness center   Mesage delivery service

4. SERVICIO DE LAVANDERIA ___   9. SERVICIO CENTRO DE NEGOCIOS ___
   Laundry service   Business center service

5. VISITO LA SALA DE ENTRETENIMIENTO   Si (Yes) ☐   No (No) ☐
   Have you visited the Entertainment Room

COMENTARIOS SALA DE ENTRETENIMIENTO - Entertainment Room comments

_____
_____
_____

ALIMENTOS Y BEBIDAS (Food and Beverage)

1. RESTAURANTE: CALIDAD DEL SERVICIO ___   4. ROOM SERVICE: CALIDAD DE LA COMIDA ___
   Los Arcos Restaurant: Service   Room Service: Food quality

2. RESTAURANTE: VARIEDAD DEL MENU ___   5. ROOM SERVICE: CALIDAD DEL SERVICIO ___
   Los Arcos Restaurant: Menu options   Room Service: Quality service

3. RESTAURANTE: CALIDAD DE LA COMIDA ___   6. BAR GLASGOW: CALIDAD DEL SERVICIO ___
   Los Arcos Restaurant: Food quality   Bar Glasgow: Quality service

Sus expectativas se cumplieron:
Totalmente ☐   Parcialmente ☐   No se cumplieron ☐

Qué le gustaría encontrar en el Hotel: _____

SUGERENCIAS (Suggestions)

_____
_____

asked to "qualify service from 1 to 10", but what does 1 mean? Is a
score of 1 good or bad?

☑ The dimensions of service respondents are asked to comment on are meaningless. Take, for example, reception service. What does reception service mean? Is the respondent being asked to comment on check-in service, check-out service, reception responsiveness, or some other dimension of performance?

◪ There is no indication of how the respondent should reply if he or she has not experienced a particular service during their stay. If the respondent does not use the fitness centre how can they "qualify" the fitness centre? If they leave the box blank, then should the person analysing the data assume the respondent did not use the fitness centre?

◪ How do the English speakers respond to questions such as "*Sus expectatives se cumplieron*"? Why have all the questions been translated, except for this one?

This may be an example of a particularly bad customer satisfaction questionnaire, but even questionnaires that have been used by well-established organisations have significant weaknesses. Albertsons, an American supermarket chain, for example, asks customers to grade on a scale of A–F (A = excellent, B = very good, C = average, D = not good, F = failed), the following service dimensions:

◪ Produce quality/freshness
◪ Meat quality/freshness
◪ Seafood quality/freshness
◪ Everyday prices
◪ Fast, friendly checkout
◪ Availability of merchandise
◪ Pharmacy prices/service
◪ Produce selection
◪ Meat selection
◪ Bakery quality/freshness
◪ Express checkout
◪ Properly bagged groceries
◪ Store cleanliness
◪ Overall grocery selection

If the checkout service is fast but not friendly, how should the respondent grade Albertsons? What does Albertsons expect individuals to take into account when they grade "express checkout"? Whether the express checkout exists? Whether it is open? Whether the express checkout

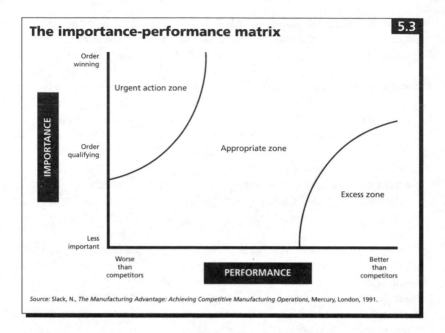

The importance-performance matrix   5.3

Source: Slack, N., The Manufacturing Advantage: Achieving Competitive Manufacturing Operations, Mercury, London, 1991.

queue length is acceptable? Whether the rule that you can use the express checkout only if you have ten or fewer items is acceptable? Even if the questions were clear, what could Albertsons do if six out of ten shoppers said that the availability of merchandise and the cleanliness of the store were average? Should Albertsons invest to improve both of these dimensions of service performance? Are they of equal importance to all customers? Perhaps Albertson's would be better advised to reduce further its prices (service dimension: everyday prices), rather than increase its product range.

These and countless other examples highlight two important factors. First, questionnaire design is a complex and subtle process. In many ways a poorly designed questionnaire is worse than no questionnaire, because it costs the organisation money and provides misleading information. Second, it is essential that customer satisfaction questionnaires identify not only how well the business is performing, but also how important each of these dimensions of performance are to the customers. Nigel Slack, professor of manufacturing policy and strategy at Warwick Business School, has developed a useful visualisation called the importance-performance matrix, which illustrates this distinction and demonstrates why it is a valuable one (see Figure 5.3).[13]

The importance-performance matrix
Before data can be plotted on the importance-performance matrix, two questions have to be addressed:

- ▪ How important is the dimension of performance being considered?
- ▪ How well is the business currently performing on the dimension of performance being considered?

Building on the work of Terry Hill, professor of operations management at London Business School, Slack suggests that importance be captured in terms of order-winning criteria, order-qualifying criteria and less important criteria.[14] Order-winning criteria are performance dimensions, such as doing things faster, better and more cheaply, that win the company business. Order-qualifying criteria are performance dimensions that have to be satisfied before the business can expect to win any orders. Television manufacturers, for example, would not win much business if the tubes in the televisions they provided never worked, or always failed within six months. Pizza delivery firms would not win orders if they were not able to deliver pizzas in less than two hours. The last set of factors, the less important criteria, neither help the business win orders, nor allow it to qualify to compete, and therefore deserve less attention and resources.

Performance is the dimension that is most frequently considered in customer satisfaction surveys. When thinking about performance it is essential to consider the organisation's position compared with the competition in the eyes of the customer. It is all very well being better than last year or the year before, but if the competition is still much better, or if your customers think the competition is much better, your business will suffer. Accordingly, it is suggested that performance is captured in terms of "better than the competition", "same as the competition" and "worse than the competition".

The strength of the importance-performance matrix becomes apparent when these two dimensions are brought together in a single visualisation (see Figure 5.3). Say, for example, that an organisation is able to deliver products much more rapidly than its competitors, and that the market values quick delivery, then delivery lead time would score highly on both scales. It is important to the customers, and the business is performing better than the competition. Hence delivery lead time would fall into the appropriate zone. Now consider brand strength. Imagine that this is unimportant in the marketplace and the company concerned has a weak brand. In this case brand strength would score low in terms of performance and low in terms of importance, thus still falling into the appropriate zone.

The other two zones, "urgent action" and "excess", are the ones that require attention. Anything falling into the urgent action zone needs to be reviewed. Customers value the dimension of performance concerned, but the organisation is not good at delivering it. Items falling in the excess zone also need attention, but of a different type. Excess means that the organisation is good at achieving the dimension of performance concerned, but customers do not value it. There are two strategies an organisation can use to deal with this: it can devote less time and less effort, thereby letting performance fall and freeing up resources to concentrate on other, more critical performance dimensions; or it can "educate" its customers and seek to convince them that they should value the "excess" dimension of performance more.

There are other issues to consider when gathering data on customer satisfaction. Two critical ones are: when to sample; and who to sample. Customer perceptions of the service they receive will be influenced not only by who they are, but also by when they are surveyed. Business class travellers or frequent fliers have different expectations of airlines than infrequent fliers. Visitors to Disneyland experience different levels of service, especially in terms of waiting in line, depending on whether they go at the weekend, during school holidays or out of season. Even on particular days there will be variations, depending on whether it is early in the morning, in the middle of the day or late at night. Surveying people only at midday may lead to a distorted picture of customer concerns.

It is also important to decide who to survey. Most organisations adopt the easy route. Hotels leave questionnaires for their guests in the bedroom. Restaurants distribute survey forms with the bill. More forward-thinking organisations realise that their target market is far larger than simply their current customers. Hence they seek to survey potential and past customers as well as present ones. They do this because they want to understand why past customers have defected and how potential customers can be converted into actual customers.

Customer satisfaction surveys: things to remember

☑ Capture both importance and performance.

☑ Remember the key measure of performance is how well the business is performing versus the competition in the eyes of the customer on those dimensions that are important to that customer.

☑ Segment the survey – identify different target groups, collect data on different days and at different times.

☑ Seek methods of capturing the views of past and potential customers, as well as present ones.

Mystery shopping and focus groups

One of the weaknesses of customer questionnaires is that they are often clinical and quantitative. Scores of six out of ten for check-in service are all very well, but they do not tell managers what to do next. Even when trend data are plotted, the only information provided is whether the organisation is getting better or worse. To gain insight into what should be done differently, qualitative descriptive data are required. These can best be collected through mystery shopping programmes and focus groups.

Mystery shoppers are widely used in the service industry by banks, restaurant chains and bars. A mystery shopper is just an anonymous customer, someone who is asked by an organisation to go and experience the service being provided and then submit feedback on it. Mystery shoppers generally concentrate on the service delivery process. When visiting a bar, for example, they would be expected to comment on:

☑ initial impressions as they walked through the door;

☑ the reception and welcome they received;

☑ the service quality – how quickly they were served, whether they were offered a range of drinks;

☑ their overall comfort and impressions – how comfortable they were, whether it was too noisy, took dark, too smoky.

☑ the reaction they received when they left – did the staff acknowledge the fact they were leaving, did they invite them to return.

Some organisations have adopted prescriptive methods of assessing these dimensions of service, often by defining explicitly the expected standards of service, such as acknowledgement within 30 seconds of walking into the bar, service within three minutes. Although such an approach simplifies data capture and analysis, it is also worth gathering information on some of the more subjective and qualitative dimensions of service performance, as these can provide further insight into the strengths and weaknesses of the operation being mystery shopped.

Mystery shopping in the strict sense is not limited to service organisations. It is possible for manufacturing firms to set up schemes where nominated customers appraise the service they receive. A novel variation on this theme is tear-down analysis of products about to be shipped, in which packed items of finished products are selected at random and stripped down. The aim of the tear-down process is to investigate in detail the product (and accompanying documentation) that was about to be shipped and hence would have been received by the customer. Any errors, omissions or defects that are found equate to those that could have been found by the customer had the product been shipped.

If even more qualitative data are required it is worth considering the use of focus groups. These are professionally facilitated discussion groups to which a cross-section of the organisation's past, present and potential customers are invited. The discussions typically last around 2–3 hours and are often conducted in the facilitator's home. The objective is to create an open and friendly atmosphere in which customers can discuss freely their expectations and perceptions of the product or service delivered. In some cases organisations have taken focus groups even further and use them to reward their most loyal customers. British Airways, for example, offers members of its frequent flier programme weekend breaks in country hotels in return for their participation in focus group discussions, which take place during the weekend.

Strategies for service recovery and customer retention

The aim of all customer satisfaction measurement methodologies is to enhance customer satisfaction and increase customer retention. Eight of the most popular strategies for achieving these ends, not already discussed, are as follows.

1 Watch the door and identify customers who have just defected or are just about to defect. For organisations such as banks and building societies this is fairly easy because they can track activity levels in established accounts and take action if these appear to be falling. For other types of organisation it is necessary to find other means of capturing the necessary data, such as loyalty schemes, monitoring credit card purchases and tracking delivery records.

2 Make it easy for customers to complain. Passive customer surveys capture only a fraction of customer frustrations. Making it easier to complain by giving out freephone numbers or providing reply paid envelopes, or even providing incentives like prize draws, increases the number of problems identified.

3 Adopt a "no quibbles" return policy. If customers are unhappy with the goods or services they have purchased accept their complaint and return their money.

4 Celebrate and communicate complaints. Eliminate people's fear that they will be punished for admitting they have made a mistake or received a complaint. Celebrate open communication of service and product failures, especially when the root cause of the failure has been found and eliminated.

5 Apologise and offer compensation to customers who have a grievance; in the right circumstances even a modest gesture can make quite a difference.

6 Explain what went wrong. Customers want to understand what went wrong, why it went wrong and what has been done to prevent the same mistake from happening again. TARP research suggests that a clear explanation of what went wrong is often more effective than simply fixing the problem.

7 Empower employees to act. Ensure that the frontline staff are given the authority to solve problems immediately. There is nothing worse than a long-drawn-out and costly complaint-handling procedure.

8 Recognise that customers are not always right; they sometimes make mistakes, but even when they do it is often because the organisation has failed to communicate with them properly. Handle these cases with sensitivity. Accept the customer's failure without recrimination and deal with the problem.

Source: Bicheno, J., *The Quality 60: A Guide for Manufacturing and Service*, Picsie Books, Buckingham, 1998.

Business performance frameworks

Other dimensions of performance should be considered when the health of a business is being checked, many of which are highlighted by the many business performance frameworks that now exist. These fall into two distinct categories: those concerned with self-assessment; and those designed to help businesses develop robust measurement systems.

Self-assessment frameworks: the Baldridge Award[15]

Global interest in self-assessment has been stimulated by the quality revolution that has affected businesses throughout the world. Over the years three self-assessment frameworks have emerged: the Deming Prize (Japan and Asia), the Baldridge Award (United States) and the European Foundation for Quality Management (EFQM) or Business Excellence Model Award (Europe). Behind these internationally recognised frameworks, however, are a host of national and regional quality awards.

As discussed in Chapter 1, the first of the internationally famous quality awards, the Deming Prize, was introduced by the Japanese Union of Scientists and Engineers (JUSE) in 1950. The second, the Baldridge Award, was created in 1987 and named after Malcolm Baldridge, an American secretary of commerce, who was a strong supporter of the award's aims and who, sadly, was killed in a rodeo accident shortly before it was launched. According to the act passed by Congress, the Baldridge Award aims to:

- Help stimulate American companies to improve quality and productivity for the pride of recognition while obtaining a competitive edge through increased profits.
- Recognise the achievements of those companies that improve the quality of their goods and services and provide an example to others.
- Establish guidelines and criteria that can be used by business, industrial, governmental and other organisations in evaluating their own quality improvement efforts.
- Provide specific guidance for other American organisations that wish to learn how to manage for high quality by making available detailed information on how winning organisations were able to change their cultures and achieve their purpose.

Awards are made annually to companies which are decreed to have achieved the highest levels of performance excellence. The criteria used to make this assessment are similar to those used in the Deming and EFQM awards, but they have evolved over the years (a summary of the 1998 criteria is given below).

Overview of Criteria for Performance Excellence

The Criteria for Performance Excellence provide organisations with an integrated, results-oriented framework for implementing and assessing processes for managing all operations. The criteria are also the basis for making awards and providing feedback to applicants. The criteria consist of seven categories:

1 Leadership. The company's leadership system, values, expectations and public responsibilities.

2 Strategic Planning. The effectiveness of strategic and business planning and deployment of plans, with a strong focus on customer and operational performance requirements.

3 Customer and market focus. How the company determines customer and market requirements and expectations, enhances relationships with customers and determines their satisfaction.

4 Information and analysis. The effectiveness of information collection and analysis to support customer-driven performance excellence and marketplace success.

5 Human resource focus. The success of efforts to realise the full potential of the workforce to create a high-performance organisation.

6 Process management. The effectiveness of systems and processes for assuring the quality of products and services.

7 Business results. Performance results, trends and comparison with competitors in key business areas: customer satisfaction; financial and marketplace; human resources; suppliers and partners; and operations.

Source: National Institute of Standards Technology home page (www.NIST.quality.gov).

The award process is straightforward and rigorous, comprising three stages of review. Before the first review all applicants complete a comprehensive self-assessment based on the award criteria. All applications are reviewed independently by members of a board of examiners. The best are selected for consensus review, which is conducted by a panel drawn from the board of examiners. They meet, evaluate the applications and decide which companies merit a site visit. The third and final stage of the review process is the site visit, the aim of which is to confirm that the original self-assessment completed by the company is valid. At each stage feedback reports, covering the quality of the submission and suggesting opportunities for improvement, are distributed to firms which fail to make the grade. A charge is made to cover the costs of processing each application ($4,500 for large and $1,500 for small companies). Considering that all applicants receive feedback reports based on at least 300 hours of review by a minimum of eight quality experts, it is easy to understand why the Baldridge feedback report has been described as "arguably the best bargain in consulting in America".[16]

Baldridge is not only about recognising excellence. It is also supposed to encourage other companies to adopt world-class quality management practices. Winners of the award (see Table 5.2) are therefore expected to act as missionaries, that is, to encourage other organisations to strive to improve their performance and quality. The 32 companies that have won awards since 1988 have taken this responsibility seriously and have, between them, delivered some 30,000 presentations on the award. Also over 1,000,000 copies of the award criteria have been distributed and more than 40 US states have established, or are now establishing, state-level award programmes, providing ample evidence of the interest the award has generated.

Two important questions about the Baldridge award remain unanswered:

- What is the impact of winning the award on the companies concerned?
- What is the real cost to the organisations that wish to apply? (The application fee ignores the effort required to put together an application.)

In terms of impact there are mixed messages. Some winners, especially the smaller companies, have commented on the number of visit requests they received following the public announcement that they had won the award. This must, of course, be traded off against the boost in reputation and brand awareness they receive. At a more detailed level there is also the question of whether winning the award actually provides competitive

Table 5.2 **Baldridge Award winners, 1988–97**

Year	Winners
1988	Commercial Nuclear Fuel Division of Westinghouse Electric Corp
1989	Milliken & Company
	Xerox Corp Business Products & Systems
1990	Cadillac Motor Car Division
	IBM Rochester
	Federal Express Corp
	Wallace Co Inc
1991	Solectron Corp
	Zytec Corp
	Marlow Industries
1992	AT&T Network Systems Group/Transmission Business Unit
	Texas Instruments Inc
	Defense Systems & Electronics Group
	AT&T Universal Card Services
	The Ritz-Carlton Hotel
	Granite Rock Co
1993	Eastman Chemical Co
	Ames Rubber Corp
1994	AT&T Consumer Telecommunications Services
	GTE Directories Corp
	Wainwright Industries Corp
1995	Armstrong World Industries Building Products Operation
	Corning Telecommunications Products Division
1996	ADAC Laboratories
	Dana Commercial Credit Corporation
	Custom Research Inc
	Trident Precision Manufacturing Inc
	Globe Metallurgical Inc
1997	3M Dental Products Division
	Merrill Lynch Credit Corporation
	Solectron Corporation
	Xerox Business Systems

Source: National Institute of Standards and Technology home page (www.NIST.quality.gov).

advantage. The response of winners is generally the same – the award does not provide any competitive advantage, but the actions that the company has taken, which have enabled it to win the award, do. Earnest Deavenport, chairman and chief executive of Eastman Chemical Company, for example, is quoted as saying: "Eastman, like other Baldridge Award winners, didn't apply the concepts of total quality management to win an award. We did it to win customers. We did it to grow. We did it to prosper and remain competitive in a world marketplace."

A similar theme emerges when considering the cost of applying. Although Xerox is rumoured to have spent $800,000 preparing its application and Corning is supposed to have devoted 14,000 labour hours to its application,[17] it appears that most award winners view the costs associated with preparing their applications as just another part of their quality programme. The process itself spurs them on to achieve higher levels of performance.

"We did not track an expense category called Baldridge application. We used the Baldridge process as an improvement tool, so investing money in those areas and processes highlighted as improvement opportunities by the assessment and feedback process was simply part of our continuous improvement process. The cost of actually preparing an application is small compared with our investments in training, process improvement and customer satisfaction. From that standpoint, we viewed the expenditure not as an expense but as an investment in our future."[18]

This quote from Raytheon raises an interesting point: companies view investments in Baldridge as investments in their future. So what is the value of these investments and what return do they deliver? To counter critics of the Baldridge award, the National Institute of Standards and Technology has sought to answer this question through its research programme. It has developed a fictitious Baldridge index based on hypothetical investments in Baldridge companies. The National Institute of Standards and Technology's press release of February 1998, reporting the results of this study, is reproduced below.

"Baldridge Index" Outperforms Standard & Poor's 500 for Fourth Year

For the fourth year in a row, the fictitious "Baldridge Index" has outperformed the Standard & Poor's 500 by almost 3 to 1, says the Commerce Department's National Institute of Standards and Technology.

The "Baldridge Index" is made up of publicly traded American companies that have received the Malcolm Baldridge National Quality Award during the years 1988–96. The National Institute of Standards and Technology "invested" a hypothetical $1,000 in each of the six whole company winners of the Baldridge Award – ADAC Laboratories, Eastman Chemical Co, Federal Express Corp, Motorola Inc, Solectron Corp and Zytec Corp. The investments were tracked from the first business day of the month following the announcement of the award recipients (or the date they began public trading) to December 1st 1997. Adjustments were made for stock splits. Another $1,000 was hypothetically invested in the Standard & Poor's 500 at the same time.

The National Institute of Standards and Technology found that the group of six outperformed the Standard & Poor's 500 by more than 2.7 to 1, achieving a 394.5% return on investment compared with a 146.9% return for the Standard & Poor's 500.

The National Institute of Standards and Technology also tracked a similar hypothetical investment in a group made up of the six whole company Baldridge Award winners and the parent companies of 12 subsidiary winners. This group of 18 companies outperformed the Standard & Poor 500 by 2.4 to 1, a 362.3% return on investment compared with a 148.3% return for the Standard & Poor's 500.

Since the past few years have been one of the stockmarket's most profitable periods in the 20th century, the National Institute of Standards and Technology also tracked an "investment" in Baldridge Award winning companies for the period starting January 2nd 1997 and ending December 1st 1997. In this study as well, the six whole company winners outperformed the Standard & Poor's 500 by 1.4 to 1, achieving a 46.3% return compared with a 32.3% return for the Standard & Poor 500.

The Business Excellence Model[19]

The European version of the Baldridge Award is the European Business Excellence Model. This was launched by the European Foundation for

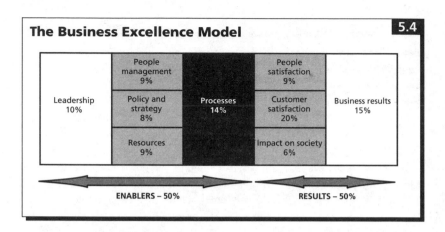

Quality Management (EFQM) in 1992, with the support of the European Commission and the European Organisation for Quality (EOQ). According to their press releases, the mission of EFQM is to:

- stimulate and assist organisations throughout Europe to participate in improvement activities leading ultimately to excellence in customer satisfaction, employee satisfaction, impact on society and business results;
- support the managers of European organisations in accelerating the process of making total quality management a decisive factor in achieving global competitive advantage.

The process of deciding who should be awarded the European prize (see Table 5.3 for the list of winners) is similar to that of deciding who should get the Baldridge Award, but the basic model differs in several ways. First, the Business Excellence Model consists of two separate sections: results and enablers (see Figure 5.4). These are designed to reflect the fact that once the necessary business enablers are in place, the results should follow. Second, the results section makes explicit reference to business results (that is, financial performance), a category many people believe should be incorporated into the Baldridge framework.

The scoring process for the Business Excellence Model is also worth reviewing. Companies are marked out of 1,000 (the actual points assigned to each category are shown in Figure 5.4). For the factors that fall within the enabler half of the model, the assessment process takes account of both approach and deployment. Approach is concerned with the

Table 5.3 **EFQM Award winners, 1992–97**

Year	Category	Company
1992	Award winner	Rank Xerox
	Prize winner	BOC Special Gases
		Industrias del Ubierna SA – Ubisa
		Milliken European Division
1993	Award winner	Milliken European Division
	Prize winner	ICL Manufacturing Division (renamed D2D)
1994	Award winner	D2D (now Celestica)
	Prize winner	Ericsson SA
		IBM (Semea)
1995	Award winner	Texas Instruments Europe
	Prize winner	TNT United Kingdom
1996	Award winner	Brisa
	Prize winner	BT
		Netas
		TNT United Kingdom
1997	Award for large company	SGS-Thomson
	Prize for large company	BT
		Netas
		TNT United Kingdom
	Award for small company	Beksa
	Prize for small company	Gasnalsa

Source: EFQM home page (http://www.efqm.org).

methods the organisation has adopted and hence concentrates on the:

- appropriateness of the methods, tools and techniques;
- degree to which the approach is systematic and prevention based;
- use of review cycles;
- implementation of improvements resulting from review cycles;
- degree to which the approach has been integrated into normal operations.

Deployment, however, is concerned with the extent to which the approach has been implemented to its full potential and therefore considers the appropriateness and effectiveness of the approach:

The West Midlands Excellence Award

SCORE	1	2	3	4	5	6
Leadership	Management act as individuals in taking and communicating decisions. They promote the need to develop and improve the organisation and to set targets.		Management act as a team, ensure two-way open communication, become involved in improvement groups. They agree plans and set priorities.		Managers develop and support improvement teams and make time available for them to work. They check progress and recognise involvement, then say "thank you".	
Policy and strategy	Partial business plans exist – concentrating only on financial targets. Plans are not widely communicated or visibly championed by the top team.		Business plans encompass data on the competition – eg, customer satisfaction measures. Key points are communicated, individuals understand and accept responsibility.		Strategic direction – vision, mission, objectives, etc are communicated to all stakeholders. A new culture is being developed. Resources are made available for continuous improvement.	
People management	Training is seen as a cost and people are employed to do a job.		The management team recognises that success comes from employees. Skills training is encouraged and training plans are agreed and aligned to company goals.		Delegation of responsibility to people at appropriate levels takes place. Appraisal schemes match the aspirations of the people and the organisation.	
Resources	Resource management tends to be directed solely at financial areas. Decisions on stock and materials are taken using hunches and "gut" feeling. Information is kept in people's heads.		Information available – often talked about or over-analysed but rarely used to improve. Cash and working capital are seen by all to be important. Stock controls are in place.		Decisions are made on the basis of information. Stock is related to customer requirements. Process improvement and evaluation of new technology takes place.	
Processes	Few procedures exist apart from financial controls. Everyone does their best and fire fighting is the norm. Changes are made to fix problems as and when appropriate.		Procedures have been written and imposed. A bureaucratic system exists with little chance for improvement. Non-conformances are seen as "bad". Systems purpose not clear to staff.		Critical processes are owned and there is support to monitor and improve them. Ownership is assigned to management who review corrective actions, etc.	
Customer satisfaction	Customer satisfaction only considered in terms of external complaints. Complaints are dealt with when they arise with little attempt to find or correct the cause.		Customer satisfaction measures are available from surveys. These data are used to set performance standards and staff have been trained in customer service.		The need to meet agreed customer needs is reflected within the core strategic plans. A customer care policy exists and is widely published.	
People satisfaction	Disputes and grievances are resolved as and when they arise. Absenteeism and/or staff turnover are high. Morale at times is poor and management tend to concentrate on themselves.		People's views are sought through surveys. Staff are consulted on improvement but grievances are dealt with by "personnel". Health and safety are treated seriously.		Two-way internal discussions take place and some form of appraisal process is used for joint improvement. Communication and feedback on a broad range of issues takes place.	
Impact on society	Environmental and social obligations seen as costly and a threat to competitiveness. Damage limitation exercises are used to counter problems.		Environmental and social requirements are dealt with to conform fully with legal requirements. Policy documents and internal standards have been written.		Strategic quality planning incorporates environmental and social obligations. Responsibility is allocated to senior managers. Environmental audits take place.	
Business results	The financial results are available and some non-financial indicators are published. They are seen as management data by the majority of staff.		Systems exist to monitor and display financial and non-financial indicators. They are communicated to staff and improvement targets are indicated.		Indicators are used to measure progress and output and are available for improvement teams. Trends are monitored and used to set targets. Suppliers' quality is measured.	

	7	8	9	10		TOTAL
Managers are willing to "let go" and empower people to become involved in improvement teams between departments and with customers and suppliers.	All managers are active inside and outside the organisation in promoting improvement activity. Continuous improvement is the culture and business philosophy.		x 10 =			
Strategic direction understood by all stakeholders. Visibly championed by top team. Key success indicators (eg, meeting customer needs) are reviewed at all levels in the organisation.	Strategic direction visibly achieved. People's success recognised by leaders at all levels. Innovation and continuous improvements in the culture and business philosophy.		x 8 =			
Employees are allowed to implement improvement activity without reference to management. A climate conducive to personal development and continuous improvement exists.	Staff morale is high and exceeds the competitive benchmark. The full potential of all people is being realised to achieve the strategic direction.		x 9 =			
All areas of waste are measured and form part of the improvement plan. Data are gathered to form an accurate view of competitors and used in business planning.	All the company's resources are deployed to meet agreed policies and strategies. Benchmarking against the "best in class" is a key resource improvement driver.		x 9 =			
Meeting customers' needs is seen as the purpose of the system. Procedures and operating standards are owned by the operators, managers and suppliers. Processes are being controlled.	System ensures all stakeholders' needs are met by existing and new products and services. Customers find it easy to do business. Continuous feedback causes improvement and innovation.		x 14 =			
Continuous research exists to identify and meet individual customer needs. This research is fully integrated into business planning, improvement and innovation processes.	Customer commitment is being delivered by all processes and relationships. Improvement and innovation exceed customers' expectations.		x 20 =			
Business changes that may adversely affect staff are jointly worked out. Data are available to show that all employees feel responsible for both their jobs and the organisation.	Benchmarking against other organisations shows employee satisfaction is high and has an improving trend. 360 degree appraisal is taken as the norm.		x 9 =			
Data show that organisation betters legal requirements. Encouragement is given for employees to become involved in supporting local community activities.	Data gathered and views sought from local society and employees and used in business planning. Formal recognition of environmental performance has been received.		x 6 =			
Benchmarking is used to compare results with industry and best in class trends. Differences between targets and results are always published and available to stakeholders on request.	The organisation's performance exceeds external benchmarks. Continuous performance improvement is part of the organisation's culture.		x 15 =			

- vertically through all relevant levels;
- horizontally through all relevant areas and activities;
- in all relevant processes;
- to all relevant products and services.

The results criteria are assessed on the basis of the degree of excellence and the scope of results presented. The degree of excellence of results takes account of:

- positive trends and/or sustained good performance;
- comparisons with own targets;
- comparison with external organisations, including competitors and "best in class" organisations (wherever possible);
- evidence that results are caused by appropriate approaches.

The scope of results takes account of the extent to which:

- the results cover all relevant areas of the organisation;
- a full range of results is presented;
- the relative importance of the results is understood and presented.

To reflect changing theories and practices the frameworks underlying both the Baldridge and the Business Excellence Awards are regularly updated. In late 1998 for example, a new version of the Business Excellence Model, making explicit mention of suppliers and organisational learning was due to be released. However, critics of these well-established quality awards comment that the application process makes them unsuitable for smaller companies or organisations with limited slack resources. In response, simplified versions of the awards have been established at national and regional levels. As already mentioned there are numerous state-level awards in existence in the United States. In the UK the British Quality Foundation (BQF) offers a national award, and groups such as Midlands Excellence offer a regional one, with a much simpler application procedure (see Figure 5.5 on the previous page). Whichever level of award an organisation decides to apply for, however, it is still expected to complete a self-assessment. Hence the spread of these awards is simply introducing more and more organisations to self-assessment, which is essentially another means of checking the health of the business.

Quick and crude health checks

As an alternative to pursuing one of the established quality awards, some organisations have decided to adopt capability maturity matrices, such as Phil Crosby's quality management maturity matrix (see Figure 5.6 on the next page).[20] Crosby's matrix consists of five stages of maturity: uncertainty; awakening; enlightenment; wisdom; and certainty. Several different dimensions of quality are also identified: management understanding and attitude; quality organisation status; problem handling; cost of quality as a percentage of sales; quality improvement actions; and summation of company quality position. For each of these a description is provided illustrating the level that a company should be at if it has achieved a certain level of maturity. For example, a company that has reached the level of awakening in terms of problem handling will "set up teams to attack major problems, but will not solicit long-term solutions". When the company has reached the stage of wisdom with regard to problem handling, however, "problems will be identified early in their development and all functions will be encouraged to suggest improvements".

Such capability maturity matrices can be used in several ways. First, they can be used as a means of self-assessment. Groups of employees can be asked to audit their own organisation or work area by ticking the boxes that most accurately describe the current status of their organisation or work area, thereby identifying opportunities for improvement. Second, groups of employees can be asked to audit other organisations or work areas. This approach still helps identify areas that require improvement, but in a more independent way which encourages transfer of working methods and practices across organisational boundaries. Third, the audits can be carried out on many units and the findings compared. Representatives from units which perform particularly poorly on particular dimensions can then be paired with those that perform well, to enable the former to learn from the latter.

Similar capability maturity grids can be, and indeed have been, developed for a great many performance and working methods and practices dimensions. These are often updated during the audit process as new and improved performance and practice standards are discovered.

5.6

Crosby's quality management maturity matrix

Quality management maturity grid

Rater .... Unit ....

MEASUREMENT CATEGORIES	STAGE I UNCERTAINTY	STAGE II AWAKENING	STAGE III ENLIGHTENMENT	STAGE IV WISDOM	STAGE V CERTAINTY
Management understanding and attitude	No comprehension of quality as a management tool. Tend to blame quality department for "quality problems".	Recognising that quality management may be of value but not willing to provide money or time to make it all happen.	While going through quality improvement programme team more about quality management; becoming supportive and helpful.	Participating. Understand absolutes of quality management. Recognise their personal role in continuing emphasis.	Consider quality management an essential part of company system.
Quality organisation status	Quality is hidden in manufacturing or engineering departments. Inspection probably not part of organisation. Emphasis on appraisal and sorting.	A stronger quality leader is appointed but main emphasis is still on appraisal and moving the product. Still part of manufacturing or other.	Quality department reports to top management, all appraisal is incorporated and manager has role in management of company.	Quality manager is an officer of company, effective status reporting and preventive action. Involved with consumer affairs and special assignments.	Quality manager on board of directors. Prevention is main concern. Quality is a thought leader.
Problem handling	Problems are fought as they occur; no resolution; inadequate definition; lots of yelling and accusations.	Teams are set up to attack major problems. Long-range solutions are not solicited.	Corrective action communication established. Problems are faced openly and resolved in an orderly way.	Problems are identified early in their development. All functions are open to suggestion and improvement.	Except in the most unusual cases, problems are prevented.
Cost of quality as % of sales	Reported: unknown Actual: 20%	Reported: 3% Actual: 18%	Reported: 8% Actual: 12%	Reported: 6.5% Actual: 8%	Reported: 2.5% Actual: 2.5%
Quality improvement actions	No organised activities. No understanding of such activities.	Trying obvious "motivational" short-range efforts.	Implementation of the 14-step programme with thorough understanding and establishment of each step.	Continuing the 14-step programme and starting Make Certain.	Quality improvement is a normal and continued activity.
Summation of company quality posture	"We don't know why we have problems with quality."	"Is it absolutely necessary to always have problems with quality?"	"Through management commitment and quality improvement we are identifying and resolving our problems."	"Defect prevention is a routine part of our operation."	"We know why we do not have problems with quality."

Source: Crosby, P., Quality is Free, New American Library, New York, 1980.

Reckitt & Colman: using maturity matrices to manage knowledge

The first pot of Colman's mustard was produced in 1814 by Jeremiah Colman at Stoke Holy Cross, a watermill near Norwich, UK. By 1850 Jeremiah had teamed up with his nephew, James, and extended the product range to include laundry blue, a starch-based cleaning agent. This brought the Colmans into direct competition with Isaac Reckitt and his Hull-based starch works.

By 1913 the businesses had begun to pool their overseas activities. They formally merged in 1938, but continued to operate almost independently until the 1970s when a more traditional corporate structure for a multinational was adopted. In an attempt to compensate for slow growth in its core markets, Reckitt & Colman had a brief but largely unsuccessful attempt at diversification in the mid-1970s. By 1980 it had become obvious that this was not going to work and that the core businesses of household and toiletries, pharmaceuticals and food could be grown. So the company rapidly divested the beer kit manufacturers, the needlework kit manufacturers, the wine makers and the jewellery makers it had acquired in the UK, the United States, Australia and New Zealand.

By 1997 Reckitt & Colman employed some 16,500 people worldwide. It made a profit of £370m on a sales turnover of some £2,200m in the 1996/97 financial year. Following the sale of its foods business, Colman's of Norwich, to Unilever, and the acquisition of Eastman Kodak's L&F Household, some 80% of Reckitt & Colman's sales are now in the household and toiletry product range. This makes it the world's fourth largest player in this market, after Procter & Gamble, Colgate and Unilever.

A new CEO: the stimulus for a new measurement system
Vernon Sankey became CEO of Reckitt & Colman on January 1st 1992, following stints as chairman and CEO of Reckitt & Colman Inc, an American subsidiary, managing director of Colman's of Norwich, and managing director in France. On becoming CEO, one of the first things Sankey asked was: "Why, if all the Reckitt & Colman businesses are broadly similar, can I not have a standard set of performance measures with which to review them?" At about the same time the then organiser of the annual operations directors conference asked Sankey if he would approve the budget for that year's conference. Sankey replied "only if I get something for it" and so evolved the Reckitt & Colman manufacturing excellence programme.

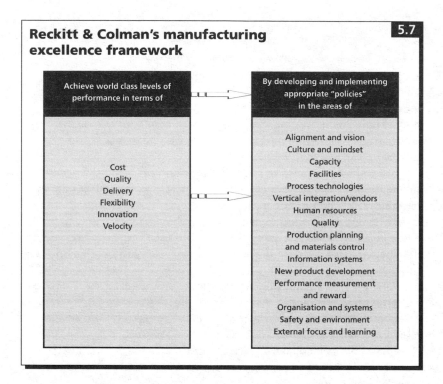

Reckitt & Colman's manufacturing excellence framework 5.7

Achieve world class levels of performance in terms of

By developing and implementing appropriate "policies" in the areas of

Cost
Quality
Delivery
Flexibility
Innovation
Velocity

Alignment and vision
Culture and mindset
Capacity
Facilities
Process technologies
Vertical integration/vendors
Human resources
Quality
Production planning
and materials control
Information systems
New product development
Performance measurement
and reward
Organisation and systems
Safety and environment
External focus and learning

Manufacturing excellence programme
The manufacturing excellence programme consisted of three main phases:

1 Education: explaining to the factory managers what manufacturing excellence was.
2 Audit: assessing where each of the businesses currently stood.
3 Action: developing and implementing action plans to move the business towards "manufacturing excellence".

Corporate management's role was to put this programme into operation by assembling the tools and techniques the businesses needed to pursue it. The task-force charged with doing this included Ted Burnside, then head of group manufacturing development, three operations directors and a university professor. According to Burnside: "The aim was to encourage each business to strive to become a stage 4 company, that is, one which seeks to gain competitive advantage through manufacturing." This was a fairly radical change given that Reckitt & Colman had traditionally been a marketing business.

Phase 1: what is manufacturing excellence?
The task-force decided that to achieve manufacturing excellence Reckitt & Colman businesses would have to achieve world-class performance in terms of cost, quality, delivery, flexibility, innovation and velocity by improving their people and processes. Figure 5.7 shows the framework they adopted, which is closely modelled on the work of Professors Hayes and Wheelwright of Harvard Business School.[21]

To explain the term "manufacturing excellence", the task-force had to define the sorts of policies a stage 4 company (that is, one seeking competitive advantage through manufacturing) would adopt. It did this by laying down the following manufacturing principles:

- Whenever possible decisions should be devolved to the level where value is added.
- Everything should be made to order, rather than to stock.
- Partnership relationships should be developed with suppliers when appropriate.
- A process of identifying the skills required for jobs at all levels of the organisation should be introduced.
- Concern for safety and the environment should be substantially increased.
- The importance of learning through benchmarking should be recognised.
- Ways of getting more accurate product costs (such activity-based costing) should be developed.

Next the task-force put together and "tested" a document consistent with these principles, which summarised the sorts of policies that stage 1, 2, 3 and 4 companies would have in place. Capacity, for example, can be broken down into a number of subdivisions, one of which is maintenance. A stage 1 company was deemed unlikely to have a maintenance programme; it would just react when machines broke down. A stage 2 company was deemed likely to have planned maintenance periods (annual shutdowns). A stage 3 company was deemed likely to have a preventative maintenance programme in place. A stage 4 company was deemed likely to have trained its operatives in preventative maintenance techniques and empowered them to maintain their own equipment.

By defining the sorts of policies stage 1, 2, 3 and 4 companies would

Extract from Reckitt & Colman's manufacturing excellence audit

5.8

		STAGE I	STAGE II	STAGE III	STAGE IV
CAPACITY	Capacity strategy	No clear capacity strategy.	Capacity designed to lag demand.	Capacity generally matches or leads demand.	Capacity always matches or leads demand.
	Investment policies	Investments as and when necessary.	Investment decisions based on capital availability.	Investment decisions designed to keep pace with technology developments.	Investment decisions based on capability requirements.
	Maintenance	Reactive maintenance strategy. Machines repaired as and when they break down.	Planned maintenance strategy. Machines maintained during annual shutdown.	Preventive maintenance strategy. Machines maintained on a scheduled basis.	Preventive and devolved maintenance strategy. Machines maintained on a scheduled basis by the operators.

Source: Ted Burnside, global supply development director, Reckitt & Colman, in a private conversation with the author.

have, the task-force built up a picture of what a world-class company would look like. This information was summarised and circulated to all the factory managers, along with instructions on how to use it as an audit (see Figure 5.8 for an extract from the audit document).

Phase 2: the audit process
The audit process was comparatively straightforward and involved three main steps:

1 Marketing representatives for each factory were asked to define what the market wanted in terms of cost, quality, delivery, flexibility, innovation and velocity. (Each marketer was given four ticks to distribute among these six dimensions for each product family.)
2 The managers of each factory were asked to identify which six of the 15 policy areas listed in Figure 5.7 on page 144 their operation needed to excel at if it was to deliver the desired performance.
3 The managers of the factory were asked to establish where their facility stood on each of these policy areas using the audit framework illustrated in Figure 5.8, thereby identifying opportunities for improvement.

Phase 3: action plans
Once the management team from a given business had completed the audit they met to:

- review the results;
- decide what their priorities were;
- develop appropriate action plans;
- identify who should be accountable for their implementation.

Outcome of the programme
The manufacturing excellence programme was piloted in 12 businesses. By late 1993 it had been extended to 21 businesses covering 50 managers in 19 countries. In total, some 61 factories went through the audit process during 1993 and as a result developed and implemented performance improvement programmes. The audit itself did not remain static during this time. One of the advantages of having 61 factories auditing themselves is that Reckitt & Colman's understanding of best manufacturing practice within the business improved immeasurably. This has made it easy for Burnside and his team to update the audit questions and identify world-class models for other Reckitt & Colman managers to visit and learn from.

The process has been so successful that in 1994 Vernon Sankey launched similar excellence programmes for the marketing and procurement functions.

Performance frameworks: the balanced scorecard

Self-assessment is undoubtedly a valuable process and the frameworks described in the previous section are among the most robust available. Returning to the doctor's analogy used at the beginning of this chapter, self-assessment is equivalent to an annual health check. Several tests are conducted in the hope that any problems, or potential problems, can be identified, but there is no specific focus for the assessment process. The alternative approach involves checking particular dimensions of health to see if any corrective action is required. So it is with businesses. Strategies are formulated. Improvement programmes are launched. One of the roles of measurement, particularly in the form of balanced measurement frameworks, is to enable progress on the various programmes and initiatives to be checked.

The most popular and widely known balanced measurement framework is the balanced business scorecard (see Figure 5.9).[22] Developed by Robert Kaplan, professor of accounting at Harvard Business School, and David Norton, president of Renaissance Strategy Group, the balanced scorecard has taken the business and consulting worlds by storm. There are several reasons for this. First, it is an idea whose time has come. Frustration with traditional measurement systems, coupled with an increasing need to cope with an ever more complex world, has created a great market opportunity. Second, it is extremely well packaged and has been carefully marketed, both by consultants and through a series of articles in the *Harvard Business Review*. Third, it appears simple, but it contains some hidden depths. The advantage of this is that people reading about the balanced scorecard for the first time can immediately understand it, but when they explore the concept in more detail they realise there is more to it than first appears.

The basis of the balanced scorecard is simple. The argument is that if an organisation has a good, well-balanced measurement system, information should be available which allows people within the business to answer four questions.

- The financial perspective: how do we look to our shareholders?
- The customer perspective: how do our customers see us?

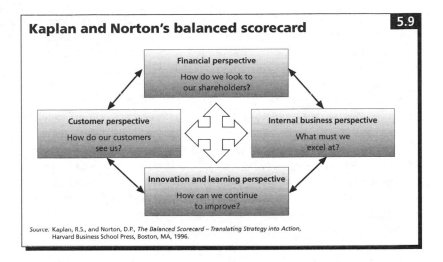

Kaplan and Norton's balanced scorecard　5.9

Source: Kaplan, R.S., and Norton, D.P., *The Balanced Scorecard – Translating Strategy into Action*, Harvard Business School Press, Boston, MA, 1996.

- ◪ The internal perspective: what must we excel at?
- ◪ The innovation and learning perspective: how can we continue to innovate and create value?

In developing a balanced scorecard Kaplan and Norton suggest that these four questions are tackled sequentially. The business must first consider how it currently looks to its shareholders and how it would like to look. Further questions to think about at this stage include:

- ◪ What are we trying to do with this business?
- ◪ Is it one we wish to invest in and grow?
- ◪ Is it one we should be milking as a cash cow?

Once these questions have been addressed it is possible to start exploring what the business should offer the marketplace in order to achieve this financial strategy. Then comes the internal perspective; what the organisation has to excel at to achieve its financial strategy and deliver value. This involves questions such as:

- ◪ How should the business be structured?
- ◪ What processes should be put in place?
- ◪ What core competencies are required?
- ◪ Which of these core competencies already exist within the business and which have to be developed?

In most organisations performance measures relating to these first three perspectives will already exist. Indeed, the primary problem in many organisations will be that too many such measures exist. One of the strengths of the balanced scorecard is that it demands that only a few crucial measures are selected. Generally, the advice given to balanced scorecard developers is that 3–5 measures should appear in each box. Hence managers are forced to select which dimensions of performance are most important in their business.

The fourth box on the balanced scorecard, which refers to the innovation and learning perspective, is the one most management teams find difficult to populate. Identifying the right measures for this box requires them to look to the future and identify explicitly how the business will continue to innovate and create value – a topic which is discussed in many organisations but rarely measured.

Scorecard criticisms

As conceived, the balanced scorecard has two weaknesses, although both can be overcome comparatively easily. The first is the emphasis on the customer perspective, which implicitly ignores the broader market perspective. What matters is not how the business looks to the customer, but how the business looks to the customer in comparison with the competition. The second, and more substantive, is the absence of any mention of suppliers. It is assumed that if the business itself excels then all will be well, but in these days of increased outsourcing, business interdependencies are continually growing, particularly in manufacturing. To overcome such shortcomings many organisations have modified the balanced scorecard for their own use (see below).

ABB's EVITA programme

ABB Sweden runs a programme called EVITA, an acronym for a Swedish phrase which means business control in the T-50 spirit. With annual sales of $35 billion and 213,000 employees around the world, ABB is one of the world's largest and most successful engineering companies. Founded in 1988 when Asea of Vasteras, Sweden, and BBC Brown Boveri of Baden, Switzerland, merged, ABB was Most Respected Company in Europe for four successive years (1994–97) in the *Financial Times*/PricewaterhouseCoopers annual survey of chief executives. ABB Sweden, with annual sales of SKr37 billion, 25,000 employees and operations in almost 200

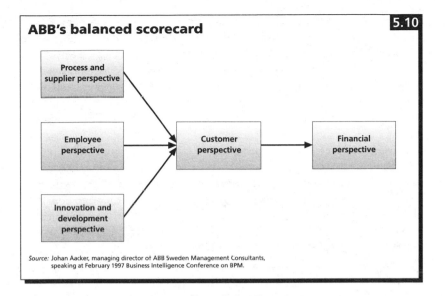

ABB's balanced scorecard `5.10`

Process and supplier perspective

Employee perspective

Innovation and development perspective

Customer perspective

Financial perspective

Source: Johan Aacker, managing director of ABB Sweden Management Consultants, speaking at February 1997 Business Intelligence Conference on BPM.

municipalities, is one of Sweden's largest engineering companies. In the early 1990s Percy Barnevick, former chairman of ABB, introduced a customer focus programme. ABB decided that to achieve customer focus it had to cut its processing times in all areas of the business and hence introduced an initiative known as T-50, the aim of which was to halve all processing times. In support of the programme, ABB Sweden's chief financial officer introduced EVITA, the underlying assumption being "you get what you measure". ABB Sweden has an internal consulting arm which was given the job of developing software tools and frameworks to facilitate EVITA. The consultants first developed their balanced performance framework, which consists of five perspectives rather than the balanced scorecard's four. These were the:

- ☑ customer perspective;
- ☑ employee perspective;
- ☑ process and supplier perspective;
- ☑ innovation and development perspective;
- ☑ financial perspective.

The logic underlying these perspectives was that to achieve financial performance you need satisfied customers. To obtain satisfied customers you need motivated employees, who can deliver the necessary products and services. Coupling these assumptions with ABB's five perspectives leads to a performance measurement framework as shown in Figure 5.10.

One of the advantages of this visualisation is that it makes explicit the time lags inherent in the balanced measurement system. Decisions taken today about innovation and development will have implications tomorrow for the range of suppliers and the forms of processes the organisation needs. Until these have been acquired and the goods produced the impact on customers and their buying behaviour will be minimal. ABB's framework can, however, be criticised for being too linear and lacking explicit acknowledgement of feedback and learning loops (for example, from customer to innovation and development, from employee to processes).

Performance frameworks for the micro level

The balanced scorecard and similar performance frameworks operate at the strategic level. They are designed to paint the big picture of the business and allow strategic health to be checked. There are, however, other levels at which health checks can be carried out, perhaps the most important being the micro process level. All operations produce and deliver goods and services through their processes. Excessive hold-ups, high levels of scrap and long lead times are all symptomatic of poorly designed processes. One of the clearest performance frameworks for dealing with these issues is one developed by Mark Brown, a US-based consultant, and explained in his book *Keeping Score: Using the Right Metrics to Drive World Class Performance*.[23] He suggests that processes are evaluated in terms of input, process, output and outcome measures. Input measures cover issues such as quality and quantity of input; process measures focus on cycle times and process parameters; output measures monitor quality and dependability of output; and outcome measures track the impact of the output (see Figure 5.11). This is best explained through a simple process example such as making a cake. The input measures would be things like quality and quantity of ingredients, for example, eggs, flour and milk. The process measures would be oven temperature and length of baking cycle. The output measures would be quality of cake, for example: does it conform to expectations, has it risen, and is the consistency appropriate? The outcome measure would be customer satisfaction: was the cake tasty, and was the customer satisfied?

The advantage of this view is that it encourages those checking the health of the business to consider the detail of the existing micro

Brown's framework of process metrics

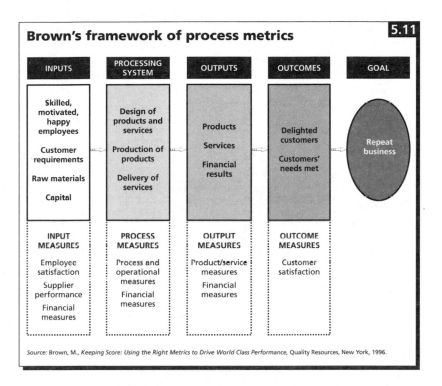

Source: Brown, M., *Keeping Score: Using the Right Metrics to Drive World Class Performance*, Quality Resources, New York, 1996.

processes. This activity complements the checks carried out by those assessing the strategic health of the business.

Checking health in practice: British Telecom

British Telecom (BT) is one of the world's largest telecommunications operators. With a global turnover of almost £15 billion and an operating profit of £3.2 billion in 1997, BT's financial health is in no doubt. Go back a few years, however, and the story is somewhat different. "In 1987 you could not open a newspaper without some horror story about our payphones not working, about lines not working. You had to wait 18 months to get a telephone line installed if you were in the City of London. Our service really was pretty awful," says Meryl Bushell, BT's head of customer service development and customer measurement.[24]

Today the situation has changed, as BT's quality of service report for April–September 1997 shows:

"86% of residential customers and 88% of business customers expressed overall satisfaction with BT and the services we provide.

Our installation service maintains its excellent record as the number of business and residential orders completed within the agreed time exceeded 98%.

Residential faults cleared in nine working hours or by successful appointment improved to nearly 82%, a rise of over 2 percentage points on the previous period. Business faults cleared in five working hours or by successful appointment remain constant at just below 89%.

Satisfaction with the Directory Assistance service (192) increased to an all time high of 91%; more calls are getting through the first time and more are being answered within 15 seconds.

Over the last six months we increased the number of payphones to 137,000, of which an average of 96% were working at any one time. This, with the increase in payment choice through the introduction of multipayment payphones and the installation of newly designed kiosks, has improved customer satisfaction with our public payphones service, now up at 90%.

Network reliability remains consistently high – fewer than one call in 200 fails because of the network and a customer is unlikely to experience a network fault more than once every seven years on any of his or her lines."

How has this turnaround been achieved and what role has been played by health checks? BT operates various mechanisms for checking health. The company has declared publicly that it is striving to win the European Foundation for Quality Management award and has twice been a prizewinner. The executive team and many of the business units operate balanced scorecards. Through a survey known internally as CARE, BT polls every employee's view of the company annually. For its largest business customers BT reviews performance quarterly through face-to-face interviews, asking customers for their views of how BT should measure itself and what performance standards it should seek to achieve. Meryl Bushell says: "What we tend to find is that once you have achieved the particular measure that the customer wanted, something else emerges as being important and so the measure sets change over time."[25] For its 6,000 or so national companies, BT runs an annual survey called the BT business class survey, which is an in-depth interview with the decision maker in each business.

For the remaining 1.4m business customers BT operates an event-driven system. This involves interviews with a sample of 11,000 customers per month, selected randomly from all those who have recently interacted with BT through the processes of provision, repair, billing, enquiry or complaint handling. The interviews, which are conducted by an external research company, consist of in-depth questions covering all aspects of the interaction the business has just had with BT, including the overall experience, the core reception, any sales activity, any engineers that visited the customer's premises and the billing process. As an example of the level of detail involved, under the heading "engineer visit" the interviewer asks whether the engineers arrived on time, whether they were smartly dressed, whether they showed their identity cards, whether they knew what they were there to do, whether they confirmed the customer's requirements, whether they checked that the customer was satisfied, whether they offered a demonstration and whether they asked if anything else was required. The large sample size means that BT is able to check the correlations between overall satisfaction and the individual experience of the customer, allowing it to isolate which factors are having the greatest positive and negative impact on overall customer satisfaction. BT is also able to distribute the results to first-line manager teams and target specific performance improvements for them. Together, these various sources of data enable BT to check health not only at the macro level, through European Foundation for Quality Management self-assessment and balanced scorecards, but also at the micro level of the service being provided by specific first-line teams.

6 Challenging assumptions

COMPARISONS are often made between a business and a living organism. Products are described in terms of a life cycle (introduction, growth, maturity, decline). Commentators talk about the birth of new industries and the death of old ones. Speaking to the Royal Society of Arts, Manufacturers and Commerce, Arie de Geus, former head of planning at Shell, posed the question: how many companies still operating today have been around for 100 years? He described some work that Shell planners had carried out to try and answer this question. They had found only about 40 large companies that had survived for 100 years, including DuPont, the Hudson Bay company, WR Grace, Kodak, and a handful of Japanese companies that could trace their origins back to the 17th and 18th centuries, Mitsui, Sumitomo and the department store Daimaru. Naturally enough, the planners next asked themselves why so few companies had survived. Given that tens of thousands of firms existed around the world in the late 19th century, why had so few managed to live as long as a human being?

"The study team found that these long-established companies had a record of adaptation to changing social, economic and political conditions and consumer needs. Each one of them had seen a lot of change ... Fundamental changes in the external world require fundamental changes in the internal structures of the company if it is to stay in harmony with that world. The history of each of those companies shows that this is what they have done ... DuPont de Nemours started out as a gunpowder manufacturer, became the largest shareholder of General Motors in the 1930s and is nowadays mostly into specialty chemicals. Mitsui's founder opened a drapery shop in Edo (Tokyo) in 1673, went into money changing and converted into a bank after the Meiji Restoration in the 19th century. The company added coal mining and towards the end of the 19th century ventured into manufacturing."[1]

Given that the pace of change today is becoming ever more rapid, it is even more important for companies to develop the ability to reinvent themselves as their markets change. Hewlett-Packard is a master at this. Today the company is recognised as one of the world's leading printer manufacturers. In the 1980s it was better known as a computer manufacturer, and in the 1970s it was one of the only manufacturers of pocket calculators. Disney's story is similar. The company started out making cartoons and films, and now operates amusement parks as well. The critical theme underlying the success of these organisations is their ability to recognise that the environment within which they are operating has changed and to reconfigure themselves accordingly. Failure to do so can have dramatic consequences.

Boiling frogs

Frogs are very slow to notice gradual changes in their environment. It is said that if a frog is dropped into a pan of boiling water it will immediately jump out. But if the frog is put into a pan of cold water which is slowly heated up, the frog will happily sit there until it boils to death.

Extending the analogy of the boiling frog to organisations immediately raises the question of how firms can monitor changes in the environment within which they are operating. At a superficial level the answer is simple: by monitoring everything in their operating environment, staying close to their customers, watching their competitors and reviewing technology trends. The rate at which the world is now changing and knowledge is being generated, however, renders this effectively impossible. There is simply too much to monitor. Hence the need for organisations to concentrate on a limited set of strategically important variables. Implicitly, this suggests that managers of organisations should regularly be asking themselves whether their strategies are still valid.

Theory of the business

There are two distinct schools of thought about strategy: the market school, popularised by Michael Porter;[2] and the competence school, popularised by C.K. Prahalad and Gary Hamel.[3] Proponents of the market-based view of strategy argue that to craft strategy, organisations should analyse the markets they are in, identify where the gaps are and seek to provide products or services which fill these gaps. Proponents of the competence view turn these arguments on their head and suggest that organisations should begin by identifying what they are good at, that is, where their competencies lie, and then seek to identify market opportunities which will allow them to exploit these competencies. In either case management, or those responsible for crafting the organisation's strategy, have to form a view of what the business is seeking to achieve. In other words, they have to develop what Peter Drucker, a management expert, calls their "theory of the business".[4] There are numerous ways in which this phrase can be interpreted, but in the context of this book it is used as shorthand for a description of the beliefs and assumptions inherent in the strategy being pursued by an organisation.

Mapping the theory of the business

The simplest way to map a management team's theory of their business is to take them through the "what-how" process. Start with two post-it notes, one labelled "what" and the other labelled "how". Stick the post-it note labelled "what" at the top of a piece of paper and ask the management team what they are trying to achieve. A typical answer might be to increase shareholder value. Record this at the top of the piece of paper and then stick the other post-it labelled "how" on to the paper. Ask the team how they are going to achieve this end. This time typical answers might include grow the value of the brands and use the assets of the business more efficiently. Record these two suggestions below the answer to the first question (increase shareholder value) and draw arrows linking the answers to the second question to the answer to the first. Then move the post-it notes down. Put the post-it labelled "what" next to one of the answers to the second question (grow the value of the brands) and put the post-it labelled "how" directly below. Now ask the team how they are going to grow the value of the brands. Once they have answered this question move the post-it labelled "what" to the other side of the picture (next to use the assets of the business more efficiently). Put the post-it labelled "how" directly below and ask the team how they are going to use the assets of the business more efficiently.

Repeat this process until a hierarchy of "whats" and "hows" of the format shown in Figure 6.1 has been constructed. Each of the arrows in this picture reflects an assumption or belief that the management team holds; for example, it is assumed that by growing the value of the brand, shareholder value will be increased; it is assumed that by convincing customers to pay premium prices the value of the brand will be increased.

Assumptions and beliefs underpinning strategies 6.1

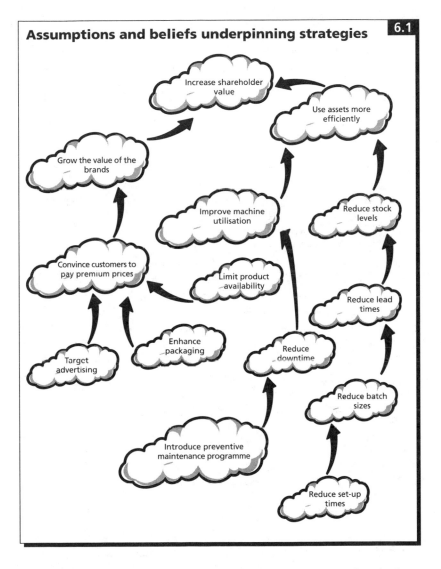

In its entirety the picture summarises the management team's theory of their business.

One of the hidden strengths of Kaplan and Norton's balanced scorecard, and indeed any balanced measurement framework, is that when used correctly it forces management teams to explore the beliefs and assumptions which underpin their strategy. This is why many commentators argue that the process of developing a scorecard is as valuable as the measures that result. Figure 6.2 shows the balanced scorecard adopted by a major pet food manufacturer. Figure 6.3 shows the same balanced scorecard redrawn in the form of a "what-how" diagram. The advantage of Figure 6.3 is that it makes the organisation's strategy more obvious. It shows that there are two basic strands to the strategy, one externally focused (the left-hand side of the figure) and the other internally focused (the right-hand side of the figure). The business is in a commodity market but seeking to improve returns. To do this, the managers have decided that they can use their internal assets more efficiently and seek to capture new market share by extending the product range. To extend the product range they need to develop new products and modify existing ones. Regarding the internal dimensions of the strategy, they have decided that the assets they should make more efficient use of are their inventories. So they are looking to their employees to come up with ideas for improved stock control and lead-time reduction.

As it stands, the balanced scorecard shown in Figure 6.2 is a reasonable first attempt. To assess its comprehensiveness, however, it is important to consider how robust is the causal relationship suggested by the link shown in Figure 6.2. Take, for example, the link between product range

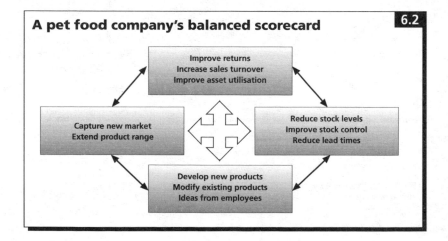

A pet food company's balanced scorecard 6.2

Improve returns
Increase sales turnover
Improve asset utilisation

Capture new market
Extend product range

Reduce stock levels
Improve stock control
Reduce lead times

Develop new products
Modify existing products
Ideas from employees

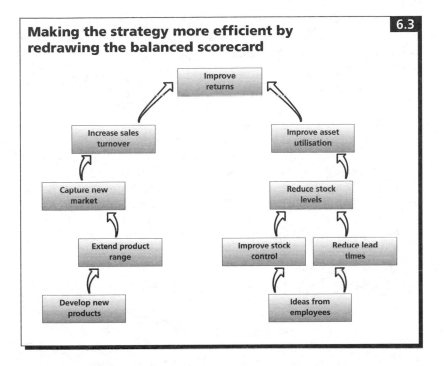

Making the strategy more efficient by redrawing the balanced scorecard

6.3

and new market. This implies that by increasing the product range new market will be captured, which is patently not the case. Increasing the product range, in itself, cannot increase market penetration. Increasing the product range might, however, attract new customers or encourage existing customers to buy more, both of which are ways new market might be captured. This highlights the fact that two extra measures are required: number of new customers; and percentage increase in purchase volumes of current customers. The question this raises is how can the pet food manufacturer develop measures (and access the data) which will allow it to assess what impact the increased product range has on customer buying patterns? With the advent of supermarket loyalty cards, the answer is reasonably straightforward. The pet food manufacturer could buy data from the supermarkets, which through their loyalty card programmes could establish whether the increased product range had changed the buying patterns of existing customers or enabled new customers to be won from the competition.

Testing the robustness of a balanced scorecard

As the discussion above implies, the "what-how" process described on page 158 can be used to test the robustness of any organisation's balanced scorecard. To do so it is necessary to redraw the scorecard in the form of a "what-how" diagram and then question whether each of the hypothesised links is valid. The question being asked is: will XYZ directly result in ABC? Take, for example, the scorecard shown in Figure 6.3. This suggests that the management team believe that ideas from employees will reduce lead times. Rephrasing the statement in the format suggested – "Will ideas from employees directly result in reduced lead times?" – immediately highlights the short-sightedness of the statement. Ideas from employees might result in reduced lead times ultimately, but only if they are focused, collected and implemented. Hence three extra dimensions can be added to the scorecard to enhance its robustness.

Double-loop learning at the strategic level

Each of the arrows in Figure 6.3 on the previous page represents a belief that underpins the management team's theory of how their business operates. Consider the theory of the business as a control panel consisting of a series of linked levers. Figure 6.3 suggests that by pulling the lever marked improve stock control stock levels will be reduced, and that by pulling the lever marked develop new products it should be possible to extend the product range. There is no guarantee, however, that any of these beliefs are valid. They make sense and seem logical, but it may be that the real key to reducing stock levels is increasing machine rates, or reducing the product range, or introducing a set-up reduction programme, which would allow batch sizes to be reduced.

Chris Argyris, professor of education and organisational behaviour at Harvard, and one of the world's leading authorities on organisational learning, has suggested that there are two types of learning: single-loop learning and double-loop learning. Single-loop learning involves the detection and correction of errors. An illustration often used is that of a simple room thermostat. If the temperature in the room falls below the desired level, the thermostat detects the error and the heating is switched on to correct it. Double-loop learning is, in many ways, more sophisticated for it involves questioning the assumptions or beliefs underlying the detected error. In the case of the thermostat this would be tantamount to the thermostat questioning why it should be set at 68 degrees. These two forms of learning can also be observed in organisations. Single-loop learning is demonstrated when the organisation is deemed not to be moving in the desired direction and some form of corrective action is instituted. Double-loop learning is exhibited when the organisation, or members of it, start to question whether the direction the organisation is moving in is the correct one. Mapping this categorisation of single- and double-loop learning back on to the three roles of measurement proposed in this book – comply, check and challenge – shows that the first two are examples of single-loop learning, where errors are detected and corrected. The third, however, is an example of double-loop learning, because in this mode of measurement data are used to explore whether the hypothesised links, which underpin the organisation's strategy, are valid.

Strategic learning in practice

Clive Jeanes, former managing director of Milliken Europe, part of the world's largest privately owned company, with interests ranging from chemicals to textiles, illustrates how he and his management team began to learn strategically as they sought to define the perfect order. In the mid-1980s Milliken Europe's internal data proved that the business had a near-perfect record for on-time delivery. Jeanes and his colleagues, however, listened to Tom Peters, a management expert, and decided that he was right when he said that it did not matter how good you thought you were, or even how good you knew you were. The only thing that mattered was how good your customers thought you were.

Grasping this message and acting on it required Milliken Europe explicitly to ask its customers how good they thought Milliken was. The company chose to do this through a customer survey conducted by an independent agency. The first survey took place in 1985 and the results were astounding. Milliken data showed that the company had a near-perfect delivery record, yet some 50% of customers complained about products arriving late. An immediate investigation was launched, and after some searching it became apparent that the reason for the discrepancy was that Milliken measured on-time delivery by checking whether the product had left its premises on time, whereas customers were interested in whether the product arrived at their premises on time. Milliken then changed its definition of on time to: does the product arrive at the customer's premises on time? As expected, this harsher measure resulted in Milliken's near-perfect record of on-time delivery evaporating, so its staff were forced to work hard to try and regain the peaks of performance they thought they had already scaled.

A year later the company commissioned another survey and once again the results were astounding, for there was still a gap between how well Milliken knew it was performing and how well customers perceived it was performing. Another investigation ensued and this time it emerged that Milliken's internal measurement system recorded partly complete shipments as on time, whereas the customer was interested in on-time delivery of the full shipment. As a result Milliken adopted a modified delivery performance measure: on time, in full (OTIF). This showed that Milliken's delivery performance was not as good as it should have been, so again its staff worked hard for 12 months to try and rectify the situation. Milliken's agency conducted another customer satisfaction survey and once again found that a gap, albeit a smaller one, existed between Milliken's actual performance and its customers' perceptions.

The story continues over several years. With each survey Milliken discovered something else that mattered to its customers but that the company was not measuring – whether the invoice was correct, whether the delivery date was a negotiated one or the one that the customer had originally requested, whether the product and packaging were error-free. Each of the customer surveys forced the management team to rethink what mattered to Milliken's customers and to challenge their own perceptions. Slowly, over a number of years, this process of continually challenging its model of the business resulted in Milliken developing what is now called the perfect order. For Milliken Europe today, a perfect order is one where:

- The customer and Milliken's sales staff agree a delivery date when the order is placed and no attempt is made by Milliken to renegotiate the date once the order has been placed.
- The product is shipped on time.
- The product is delivered on time.
- The correct quantity of product arrives.
- The product is of the correct quality when it arrives.
- The packaging is correct.
- The accompanying documentation is error-free.
- The accompanying documentation is mailed on time.
- The customer makes no other complaints.
- The invoice is paid on time.

One of the most interesting elements of this definition is the last one, which emphasises that the order is not perfect unless the customer pays on time. In Milliken's experience this is a valid measure, and Jeanes reports that the company experienced a reduction in debtor days outstanding following the introduction of the perfect order.[5]

Milliken's story, however, does not end there. Once the business had developed the concept of the perfect order and started to work with it, managers noticed that customer satisfaction was a predictor of future financial performance. Jeanes describes the breakthrough as follows:

"Perhaps the biggest breakthrough of all came with our understanding of how good a prediction of business performance the customer surveys were. It took 5–6 years to see it, but then a clear pattern started to emerge. There was a correlation between the survey findings and financial results, but with a time lag of about 18–24 months. This meant that if a survey showed a downward trend, compared with prior years, the business could expect to lose sales, market share and profit within 1–2 years. Equally, where there were improving trends in the survey, the sales and profit figures would in due course reflect this."[6]

The essence of learning strategically is building an explicit model, a theory of the business, which can be used to make predictions, and then continuously challenging this model, either with hard facts or figures, such as those collected by Milliken, or through structured debate. An example of the latter approach is provided by Alan Meekings, a vice-president of Gemini Consulting, who constructed what he calls a visible indicator tree while working with Network SouthEast, one of the UK's regional rail companies.[7] The visible indicator tree (see Figure 6.4 on the next page) makes explicit the linkages between one of Network SouthEast's overriding strategic business objectives – "92% of trains to arrive within 5 minutes of published time" – and lower-level actions, such as minimise wheel lathe downtime. The strength of this visualisation is that it highlights practical steps that can be taken to achieve the strategic objective. It also facilitates organisational alignment behind these steps by showing everyone where they fit in the big picture, and makes explicit the assumptions or beliefs that underpin the implementation process. By reducing wheel lathe downtime it should be possible to achieve the target for percentage wheel sets to plan. This should enable the target for percentage trains pending wheel sets to be attained, which will ensure the percentage trains non-operational target

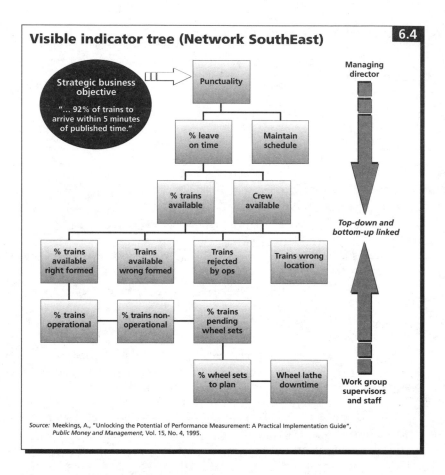

Visible indicator tree (Network SouthEast) 6.4

Strategic business objective

"... 92% of trains to arrive within 5 minutes of published time."

Punctuality

% leave on time

Maintain schedule

% trains available

Crew available

% trains available right formed

Trains available wrong formed

Trains rejected by ops

Trains wrong location

% trains operational

% trains non-operational

% trains pending wheel sets

% wheel sets to plan

Wheel lathe downtime

Managing director

Top-down and bottom-up linked

Work group supervisors and staff

Source: Meekings, A., "Unlocking the Potential of Performance Measurement: A Practical Implementation Guide", *Public Money and Management*, Vol. 15, No. 4, 1995.

is not exceeded, and so on. Only by making these linkages explicit can their validity in practice be tested.

Strategic learning at Sears[8]

The worst year in the history of Sears Roebuck, a US retailing firm, was 1992. On sales of $52.3 billion, the company's net loss was $3.9 billion, almost $3 billion of which came from the merchandising group. Over the next five years Sears sold off all its non-retailing businesses, closed 113 stores and thoroughly renovated the 800 mall-based stores that remained, at a cost of $4 billion. The 101-year-old Sears catalogue, which was losing $100m a year, was closed down.

"Store operations were re-engineered. Staffing was adjusted to put more of the best people in the stores during evenings and weekends, when the best customers were shopping ... The results were spectacular. In 1993 the company's merchandising group reported new income of $752m, a sales increase of more than 9% in existing stores, and market share gains in apparel, appliances and electronics. Sears as a whole had one of its most profitable years ever. The resurrection produced a total shareholder return for the year of 50%."

The danger was that these results were so good that people might have sat back and relaxed, thinking they had solved the company's problems. To avoid this trap Arthur Martinez, chief executive of Sears, established the Phoenix team, which consisted of the company's 150 most senior managers. Initially, their remit was defined as to "make Sears a compelling place to shop". Workgroups followed, benchmarking took place, focus groups with customers were held, vision and values were defined. The Phoenix group members developed their own identity and extended their remit. They wanted to make Sears not only a compelling place to work, but also a compelling place to shop and a compelling place to invest. They also wanted evidence that they were succeeding, not in the traditional sense of having a set of measures which allowed them to monitor progress, but in the sense of having a clear, demonstrably valid, explicit theory of the business.

"We formed a new team to convert these measures into an econometric model. The measurement team's task was to come up with a kind of balanced scorecard for the company – the Sears Total Performance Indicators, or TPI. But we wanted to go well beyond the usual balanced scorecard, commonly just a set of untested assumptions, and nail down the drivers of future financial performance with statistical rigour. We wanted to assemble the company's vast body of interview and research data – some of it from task-forces, much of it collected routinely over the course of the years but never used strategically – then analyse it, draw connections across the data sets, and construct a model to show pathways of actual causation all the way from employee attitudes to profits (see Figure 6.5 on the next page)"

Constructing the model involved copious amounts of data collection and testing. New measures had to be defined and new data gathered, as Sears had never before measured items such as "personal growth and

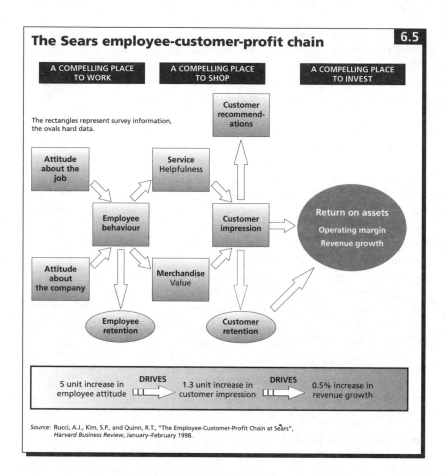

The Sears employee-customer-profit chain 6.5

A COMPELLING PLACE TO WORK **A COMPELLING PLACE TO SHOP** **A COMPELLING PLACE TO INVEST**

The rectangles represent survey information, the ovals hard data.

Customer recommendations

Attitude about the job

Service Helpfulness

Employee behaviour

Customer impression

Return on assets
Operating margin
Revenue growth

Attitude about the company

Merchandise Value

Employee retention

Customer retention

5 unit increase in employee attitude **DRIVES** 1.3 unit increase in customer impression **DRIVES** 0.5% increase in revenue growth

Source: Rucci, A.J., Kim, S.P., and Quinn, R.T., "The Employee-Customer-Profit Chain at Sears", *Harvard Business Review*, January–February 1998.

development" or "customer retention". For the first two quarters of 1995 Sears staff collected data, both old and new. In the third quarter they sent all their data to a firm of econometric statisticians, who analysed it and identified the most significant relationships. Adjustments to the model were made, further data were collected and further analyses were undertaken.

"It was exciting stuff. We could see how employee attitudes drove not just customer service but also employee turnover and the likelihood that employees would recommend Sears and its merchandise to friends, family and customers. We discovered that an employee's ability to see the connection between his or her work and the company's strategic objectives was a driver of positive behaviour. We learned that asking customers whether Sears is a 'fun place to shop' told us more than a long list of more specific questions would. We were also able to establish fairly precise statistical relationships. We began to see exactly how a change in training or business literacy affected revenue."

Sears's managers freely admit that their employee-customer-profit chain model is not perfect and openly say that they doubt it ever will be. They also, however, make the important point that they now understand more about the business than they did before.

"The point is that we know vastly more than we once did. Take the example about the quality of management as a driver of employee attitudes. Our model shows that a 5 point improvement in employee attitudes will drive a 1.3 point improvement in customer satisfaction, which in turn will drive a 0.5% improvement in revenue growth. If we knew nothing about a local store except that employee attitudes had improved by 5 points on our survey scale, we could predict with confidence that if revenue growth in the district as a whole were 5%, revenue growth at this particular store would be 5.5%. These numbers are as rigorous as any others we work with at Sears. Every year, our accounting firm audits them as closely as it audits our financials."

Telling stories and drawing pictures

The essence of strategic learning was earlier identified as building an explicit model of the business and then rigorously testing it. Sears has certainly achieved this, but the Sears story also highlights a further important facet of strategic learning, that of telling stories. The ability to weave a story around the executive team's business model is essential, not only so the model can be communicated, but also so its comprehensiveness can be assessed. An appropriate analogy would be that of lawyers or detectives, for they both have to build cases (to tell stories) based on limited available data. They do so by investigating, by collecting facts, by pooling these facts and putting forward hypotheses, which they then destructively test to assess their validity. The aim of their detective work is to create a believable (preferably valid) explanation for a series of events. Medical scientists have the same role. One of the earliest examples of medical science at work is provided by the story of a cholera outbreak in London in the early part of the 20th century. Several people residing

London cholera outbreak 6.6

⬤ Water pump
⊞ Cholera cases

within a block of each other died from the disease in close succession, which suggested that the source of the disease was somewhere in the locality. The medical examiner's breakthrough came when a wealthy woman, who lived several blocks away, also caught the disease. It emerged that every day she rode along the street where most of the victims lived and frequently stopped at their water pump for a drink. The thing that linked all the victims was the fact that they had all drunk water from the same pump. Hence the source of the cholera was identified.

There are two important messages in this story. The first is the power of visualisation in prompting people to challenge their assumptions. In the case of the cholera outbreak, a picture showing the streets where the various victims lived immediately causes the viewer to ask what it is that links all of these people together (see Figure 6.6). The nature of the visualisation immediately draws the viewer's eye to the central point, which is where the water pump was situated.

The second is that qualitative as well as quantitative data have roles to play when managers are challenging their theories of the business. Quantitative data, such as those collected through customer surveys and loyalty schemes, are valuable if the theory is to be formally tested. Qualitative data, however, are equally valid if the aim is to challenge the robustness of the model. Rarely do managers change the way they operate, or revise their organisation's strategy, solely on the basis of statistics. Much more common is the gradual absorption of facts, figures, opinions and observations, all of which come together and gradually result in the realisation that not everything is as it should be. Such critical reflection, however, does not always occur naturally in organisations. It is often worth facilitating the process, both explicitly and implicitly. Explicit facilitation can involve formal meetings and discussions, where the main agenda item is the validity of the executive team's business model. Implicit facilitation involves establishing environments which encourage critical reflection.

Organisations are increasingly assimilating this message. Hot desking, a system in which people do not have a fixed place of work, is becoming more common. Where this has been adopted employees are offered a choice of work zones designed to reflect the fact that at different times of the day, or while different tasks are being undertaken, different work settings are more or less appropriate. Reflective rooms, modelled on libraries, or creative rooms, full of garish colours and white light, are becoming common. Sun Microsystems, in Silicon Valley, hangs electronic whiteboards on the walls in its corridors. The rationale for this is twofold. First, people can schedule short meetings for corridors. Since there are no chairs and desks available, such meetings are unlikely to last for a long time. Second, there is a high probability that someone not intimately involved in the subject being discussed will pass by, join the discussion for a few minutes, perhaps offer an alternative view or solution and then move on. This maximises the chance of a random creative encounter, which research has shown results in a far higher proportion of creative ideas than a planned meeting. BMW-Rolls-Royce Aerospace, at its new development and test facility in Dahlewitz, near Berlin, has adopted a similar strategy. The BMW-Rolls-Royce facility consists of three hexagonal office blocks connected by horizontal glass walkways. Although traditional departments exist, people do not sit in departmental groups but are dispersed throughout the building. Furthermore, there is only one photocopier and one kitchen on each floor. Despite the inconvenience caused, these three design features (random seating, one photocopier, one kitchen) have been deliberately adopted to force employees to move around the building, thereby increasing the likelihood of chance creative encounters.

Some organisations have gone even further and established alternative workplaces designed to provoke creative thinking. Skandia, a Swedish insurance company, has established several futures centres – hideaways in the Swedish countryside where cross-cultural task-forces meet to explore and seek to understand what the future might hold for Skandia. The first such centre, Villa Askudden, was opened in 1997. Five Skandia Futures Teams have been established, consisting of diverse members from different generations, professional backgrounds, functions and cultures. Each team's task is to understand the impact a different facet of the future is likely to have on Skandia and the markets in which is it operating, for example, technology, population trends and market trends.

Five simple strategies to ensure assumptions are challenged

1. Play devil's advocate
Introduce formal strategy challenge sessions where different groups of managers are explicitly asked to argue the same case from different angles. Set up the debate so that each side has to contradict the other and has to provide data to support the arguments they are putting forward.

2. Ask customers and frontline staff
Customers and frontline staff often have very different views from the management team of the validity of the organisation's strategy. Video-taped interviews with customers and frontline staff played back at the start of strategy challenge sessions have proved to be valuable ways of opening up the debate and forcing managers to think the unthinkable.

3. Expose differences of opinion
Ask members of the management team to say how the business is competing in terms of quality, speed, dependability, flexibility and cost, and then ask them to apportion 100 points among these dimensions to reflect the importance of the various parameters to the organisation. The differences in perception can be startling, and the subsequent discussion can identify some serious shortcomings in the organisation's strategy.

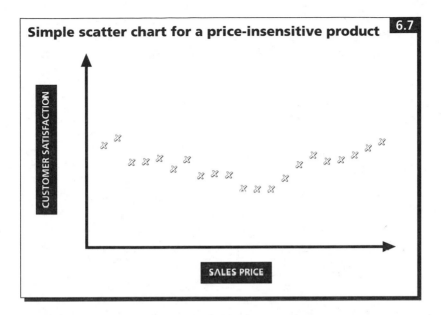

Simple scatter chart for a price-insensitive product 6.7

CUSTOMER SATISFACTION

SALES PRICE

4. Adopt measles charts
Record the root causes of product and service failures on business process maps by putting red stickers for each and every root cause. The resultant measles diagrams, that is, process maps covered in red spots, make obvious the shortcomings in the organisation's business processes.

5. Conduct quick and crude correlations
Choose two dimensions of performance that everyone believes are related and plot them on a scatter chart (see Figure 6.7 for an example). The analysis is not particularly scientific, but the chart soon highlights whether or not there appears to be a relationship between the two dimensions of performance.

The power of data

So far this chapter has discussed the development of explicit business models or explicit theories of how businesses operate. Pooling qualitative data can certainly generate such models, but quantitative information also has a role to play. This raises two questions: Where do the necessary data come from? How can they be analysed? The Sears case provides some insight into the answers to these questions, because Sears was able to capture the data it required using surveys, focus groups and mystery shoppers and analyse them using well-established econometric methods. There are, however, numerous other valuable data sources. Amazon Books, one of the most well-established e-commerce retailers, explicitly uses previous customers' purchasing habits to try and predict which books new customers might like to purchase. Search for Kaplan and Norton's book, *The Balanced Scorecard – Translating Strategy into Action*", on Amazon's web page and a message will flick across your screen saying:

"Check out the following titles! Readers who bought *The Balanced Scorecard – Translating Strategy into Action* also bought: (i) *Leading Change* – John B. Kotler; (ii) *Competing for the Future* – Gary Hamel and C.K. Prahalad; and (iii) *Cost and Effect: Using Integrated Cost Systems to Drive Profitability and Performance* – Robert S. Kaplan and Robin Cooper"

Tesco, a leading British supermarket chain, knows that men who buy nappies on Friday evenings also often buy beer. Airlines, through their frequent flier programmes and alliances with hotels and car rental agencies, can establish what percentage of flights a passenger takes are taken with them. Data mining, that is, exploring the links between buying habits and spending patterns, has become a big business. Take supermarkets, for example. With their loyalty schemes they are able not only to monitor people's buying patterns, but also, in theory, to predict when they will shop, what they will buy and what money-off vouchers they could be sent to encourage them to shop at a particular store. The data gathered also furnish the retailer with insights into changes in consumer spending patterns following the introduction of new products. If Ben and Jerry introduce a new type of ice-cream, retailers can tell Ben and Jerry whether they are winning business from their competitors with their new products. Loyalty schemes are not the only source of valuable data for these purposes. At a conference in 1997 Meryl Bushell, head of customer service development and customer measures at British Telecom, explained that the company's research into the drivers of customer loyalty has changed its assumptions about the levels of service it needs to deliver to customers:[9]

"Initially, we set our target levels at the 7 plus level. We were aiming for satisfaction. Satisfied customers, however, are not particularly loyal to you. We've had some research done recently which shows of our own customer base, where we've asked the 'loyalty' and 'would you recommend' types of questions, of the customers who are satisfied only about 9% are actually loyal to us. To get real loyalty from our customers we need them scoring us 9 or 10 out of 10."

Because of the volume of data that British Telecom collects through its customer satisfaction survey, like Sears it has been able to construct a generic model which identifies what British Telecom has to do if it is to delight its customers.

"There is a hierarchy of things you need to do to reach the delighted level. We've found that with the customers who are dissatisfied with us – totally dissatisfied with us – [the problem] tends to be that we are not meeting their basic requirements of reliability. At the level above that, to start moving into the real satisfied area, you need to be reliable in terms of the people commitments you give as well as the product or solution that you are delivering. To start moving into the area where the customer is more than just averagely satisfied you have to have the levels of flexibility and responsiveness that the customer is looking for in terms of how quickly you can do things and how flexible you are to their requirements. To really get to the delighted customer, on top of that you have to build the trust, relationship and empathy because people buy from people."

The theme underlying Bushell's comments and those from representatives of Sears is the power of data. Far too often organisations spend inordinate amounts collecting data which, at best, they then use to check the health of the business, that is, to establish whether they are achieving the objectives they set out to achieve. Rarely do they make full use of these data and use them to challenge the basis of the organisation's strategy and the beliefs and assumptions that underpin it, which is exactly what the most enlightened organisations are doing explicitly, continuously and systematically. Gone are the days for these organisations of managing solely by gut feelings – they have entered the phase of fact-based management.

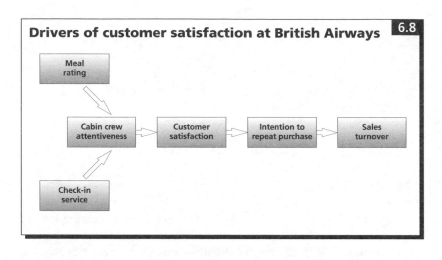

Drivers of customer satisfaction at British Airways 6.8

Strategic learning at British Airways[10]

British Airways carries some 35m passengers per year. Turnover for the 12 months ending March 31st 1998 was £8,642m, which resulted in a profit before tax of £580m (9.4% higher than in the previous year). Senior managers argue that the airline's record of success has been built on high quality service provided by a dedicated workforce, combined with marketing and continued cost reduction. To enable them to maintain and monitor the quality of service delivered, British Airways and its agencies interview approximately 500,000 passengers per year. The airline's approach to the measurement of customer satisfaction is rigorous. Random samples of passengers are selected and asked to complete questionnaires or engage in face-to-face interviews. Both the questionnaires and interviews are structured around the way in which customers are processed by the airline. Hence customers are first asked about check-in and only later about the flight itself. Under the heading "check-in" they are asked about check-in service: was it efficient; was the waiting in line acceptable; were the check-in staff friendly; were they helpful; did they use the customer's name? Next they are asked about the flight: were the cabin crew attentive; did they anticipate the customer's needs; how was the aircraft interior; how was the meal? Lastly they are asked about their overall impressions of the flight: were their expectations met; will they fly with British Airways again; would they recommend the airline to a friend?

British Airways has been collecting these data since the early 1980s so it now has a substantial data set. Preliminary research using these data has been able to demonstrate that customer satisfaction is correlated with sales turnover, through an intervening variable, intention to repeat purchase. The data also suggest that the major driver of customer satisfaction is cabin crew service, which in turn is driven by check-in service and meal rating (see Figure 6.8). These findings are logical, in that the first contact many passengers have with the airline is at check-in. If the check-in process is efficient and the staff helpful, the passengers are likely to board the plane in a positive frame of mind. Another major contact with the cabin crew is when the meal is served. Hence it is not surprising that meal rating is a driver of cabin crew attentiveness. If confirmed, however, these findings have significant implications for British Airways. Traditionally, senior managers in the company have assumed that overall customer satisfaction is a function of all the interactions passengers have with the airline: check-in service; departure time; aircraft interior; cabin crew service; meal rating; arrival time; and baggage reclaim. If, as the preliminary data suggest, cabin crew service really is the major driver of overall customer satisfaction, one of the implications is that the airline should consider focusing its effort on improving cabin crew service, perhaps at the expense of some of the other listed dimensions of performance.

7 Benefiting from measurement: a summary

O RGANISATIONS all over the world are reviewing and improving their measurement systems. They are doing so because managers want better methods of establishing position, monitoring progress, motivating and rewarding people, making decisions, understanding the needs of their customers and responding to the challenges posed by the actions of their competitors. In Chapter 3 many reasons for measuring performance were identified. It was suggested that these could be clustered under four headings, the 4 CPS of measurement: check position; communicate position; confirm priorities; and compel progress. The 4 CPS are the basic reasons why people measure, but it is only when an organisation has the necessary processes in place to allow each of the three roles of measurement covered in Chapters 4, 5 and 6 to function effectively that it is able to gain the full benefits.

The first role of measurement: comply

In all organisations there are certain performance parameters which can be described as non-negotiable. Airlines cannot afford to have near misses or infringe noise level restrictions. Restaurants cannot afford to have repeated outbreaks of food poisoning among their clientele. Privatised water companies cannot afford to lose too much water through pipe leakage, given current water reserves and the regulator's interest in leakage figures. Failure to achieve adequate performance across any of these dimensions can result in sanctions for either the business or the individual members of the organisation. In extreme cases the organisation, or the individuals within it, can forfeit their licence to operate. Union Carbide came close to this following the Bhopal chemicals disaster. Early in the morning on December 3rd 1984, 27 tonnes of a highly toxic gas, methyl isocyanate, leaked from the Union Carbide pesticide factory in Bhopal.[1] Reports suggest that of the 800,000 people living in the city at the time, 2,000 died immediately, 300,000 were injured and 8,000 have died since. Subsequent investigations have revealed that the leak was caused by a series of mechanical and human errors. Part of the plant's safety equipment had been non-operational for four months and the rest failed.

Although it denied liability, Union Carbide agreed to a settlement of $470m in the Indian Supreme court in 1989. The impact of this episode on the business has been massive. In 1984 Union Carbide employed 98,400 people; today it employs fewer than 12,000. Sales plummeted from $9.9 billion in 1980 to just over $6 billion in 1996. In December 1985 the company became the target of a hostile takeover bid by GAF Corporation. In response, Union Carbide sold its consumer products group, including Glad garbage bags, Eveready batteries and Prestone anti-freeze, and bought back 56% of its stock, thereby taking on a $3.3 billion debt. Since then Union Carbide has spun off its pesticides business, its graphite electrodes business, its silicones business and, in 1992, Linde, its industrial gases unit.

So how can organisations use their performance measures to ensure that the non-negotiable performance parameters are not infringed? In this context the organisation's measures are effectively a radar system. They are designed to provide an early-warning signal that something is about to go wrong and that corrective action should be taken. Imagine, for example, the rate at which pressure builds up in a nuclear pressure vessel. If it builds up too rapidly an early-warning signal is required so that corrective action can be taken to remedy the situation. At the organisational level an equivalent example might be public opinion. Shell's brand and revenue, for example, were both damaged by bad publicity about the organisation's policies in Nigeria and its plans to dispose of an obsolete oil rig by sinking it in the North Sea. The company's licence to operate was not revoked, but the failure to monitor, anticipate and manage public opinion was damaging none the less.

The second role of measurement: check

When politicians talk about the health of the economy they are selective about which figures they use. Members of one party may focus on the balance of payments, while those from another will point to interest rates. But looking at a single dimension does not provide an accurate reflection of the health of any system, whether it is an economy, a hospital or school, or a business. What is required is a balanced set of measures. In business it is reasonably widely accepted that such a balanced perspective can be achieved if measures are derived from strategy and allow the following questions to be answered:[2]

- How do we look to our shareholders?
- How do we look to our customers?

■ What must we excel at internally?

■ How can we continue to innovate and create value?

Underpinning this set of questions is the assumption that a balanced set of measures, derived from the organisation's strategy, allow the implementation of that strategy ot be monitored.[3]

The third role of measurement: challenge

Strategies, however, consist of a series of linked assumptions or hypotheses. It is assumed that if delivery performance improves, customer satisfaction will increase, and if customer satisfaction increases the number of repeat purchases will increase. But there is no guarantee that these assumptions stand up. Testing their validity is the third role of measurement. Here the aim of the review process is to explore whether the assumptions underpinning the strategy hold. In effect, the question being asked is not is our strategy being implemented, but is our strategy correct? In academic terms this distinction is basically the same as the one between single- and double-loop learning.[4] Single-loop learning is concerned with corrective action. It involves identifying whether there are any deviations from plan and then correcting them. This is effectively what happens in the second role of measurement, check health. Double-loop learning is different. It requires the assumptions underlying the plans to be questioned. It relies on people challenging the accepted values and norms by asking: are our plans correct?

The three roles: a prescriptive approach

What are the implications of the observation that there are three fundamental roles of measurement: comply, check and challenge? To answer this question it is necessary to examine the differences between the three roles of measurement and establish how these might surface in a practical setting. As suggested in Chapter 1, performance measurement involves acquiring, collating, sorting, analysing, interpreting and disseminating performance data. The data are collected via customer opinion surveys, focus groups, complaint analyses, labour records, quality records, and so on; then they have to be collated. If 73 people visiting a restaurant complete its customer satisfaction survey, someone has to take the 73 responses and pool the data, converting them from individual responses into a meaningful data set. Simply creating the data set, however, is not enough, for next the data have to be analysed. Someone, or perhaps several people, has to review the data set and try to understand what messages it contains for the organisation. Then the messages have to be communicated. Groups of people have to come together and decide whether the messages extracted from the data set are valid, and, if so, how they should be acted upon.

The first three processes – data acquisition, collation and sorting – are mechanistic. No matter what the type of data or how they are to be acquired, someone must physically collect and gather them together (collate them) before anything else can be done. The other three processes vary, however, according to the role of measurement being employed. Different analysis, interpretation and dissemination processes are required when using measures as a means of ensuring compliance against critical performance parameters than when using them as a means of challenging assumptions. In the first case, the review processes must not only provide an early-warning signal, but also ensure there is enough time for corrective action to be taken. Generally, such early-warning signals should be close to the point of process control. Individuals responsible for the processes must have the authority to act on the signals when they receive them, rather than waiting for approval from some other part of the organisation.

Checking health is different. The review process is likely to be scheduled and formal. In most organisations health checks take place regularly, rather than in response to impending crises. The entire senior management team is likely to be involved. The discussion is likely to be well structured and to follow a similar format every time. Multiple measures will be considered and reasons for performance shortfalls discussed. The review process most appropriate for the third role of measurement, challenge, is different again. Discussions are likely to be less frequent, perhaps once a quarter as opposed to once a month, which might be more appropriate for the health checks. Senior management will still be involved, although there may be a role for others in the review process. The aim of the review is to challenge both conventional wisdom and assumptions about the way that the business is working. Simply involving the people who developed and have signed up to the strategy may stifle this debate. Hence there may be a need to involve outsiders, frontline staff or even customers. The setting for the review is likely to be informal, perhaps off-site and out of normal working hours. The atmosphere needs to encourage "out of the box" thinking. This can be difficult to achieve in most board rooms, which are generally loaded with symbolism.

Figure 7.1 on page 183 provides more structure to these issues by comparing and contrasting possible forms of review process for the three roles of measurement.

The three roles: an alternative perspective

The framework outline in Figure 7.1 is one way of viewing the three roles of measurement. For some organisations this will be appropriate and they will want to establish distinct review processes which operate on different time cycles: a continuous process for ensuring compliance; a monthly process for checking health; and a quarterly process for challenging assumptions. For other organisations the notion of a management team sitting down once a quarter and challenging the assumptions underpinning their strategy will be an anathema. The issue, then, is not that everyone should adopt the three performance review processes outlined above, but that all managers should question whether these three processes exist, in some form, in their organisation. When did the management team last sit down with real data to challenge the assumptions underpinning the strategy? When did the management team last commission the analysis to explore whether any correlations exist between the different dimensions of business performance? How widespread is agreement in the organisation about the non-negotiable performance parameters? People may know what the parameters are, but what systems exist to provide an early warning that one or more of the non-negotiable parameters may be about to be infringed?

The three roles and the 4 CPs

To assess the quality of a given organisation's measurement systems and review processes it is necessary to return to the 4 CPs of measurement and explore them further. The 4 CPs are essentially sequential. Position has to be checked before it can be communicated. Plans and priorities cannot be confirmed until performance data have been shared. Progress cannot be compelled until priorities have been defined. It is important to bear this in mind as it implies that however an organisation chooses to use its measures, it should design systems which allow position to be checked and communicated, priorities to be confirmed and progress to be compelled. The theme of this book has been that there are three different ways in which organisations can choose to use their measurement systems – the three roles of measurement. But how do these three roles map on to the 4 CPs?

The 4 CPs in comply

The aim of the compliance role of measurement is to ensure that the organisation never infringes any of its non-negotiable performance parameters. Hence the first task of a compliance-based measurement

The three roles of measurement

7.1

	Aim of the review	COMPLY *To establish whether any of the non-negotiable performance parameters are in danger of being infringed*	HEALTH CHECK *To assess whether the long-term viability of the business is under threat*	CHALLENGE *To challenge the assumptions underpinning the strategy of the business and to establish whether they are still valid*
OUTPUTS	What outputs are being sought?	Warning <> non-negotiable parameter is in danger of being infringed	Warning <> long-term health of the business is under threat	Warning <> assumptions underpinning the strategy are invalid
PROCESS	What form will the review take?	Continuous process	Structured meeting	Unstructured discussion
	How often will the review take place?	By exception reporting	Monthly	Quarterly
	How long will the review last?	Minutes to hours	Up to four hours	All day (sometimes longer)
INPUTS	Which measures should be considered?	Single measures	Balanced set of measures	Multiple measures
ACTORS	Who are the main actors in the review process?	Those directly concerned with performance parameter at risk	The senior management team for the business	The senior management team + strategic planners + facilitator + others (eg, those willing – and able – to challenge the strategy… might include frontline staff)
	What are their respective roles?	To solve the problem – ie, ensure the infringement does not occur	To carry out the health check. Identify any threats to the long-term health of the business and propose corrective actions	Participants – to challenge the assumptions underpinning the strategy using real data rather than "feel". Facilitator – to keep the participants honest, ie, point out when they are not basing their arguments on data
CONTEXT	Most appropriate environment?	Action oriented	Professional and focused	Reflective and discursive
	Why do we want this sort of environment?	Need to solve the potential problem quickly	Want to be thorough, but complete review relatively rapidly	Want to challenge basis of strategy. Identify alternative reasons for patterns in data
	Where should the review take place?	As close to the potential problem as possible	Formal setting – place of authority	Offsite, neutral location
	When should the review take place?	As soon as the potential problem is flagged	During normal working hours	Outside normal working hours

system must be to check the organisation's position against those parameters that have been identified as critical. As already discussed, this checking process should, in most cases, be continuous. Infringements of non-negotiable parameters can occur at any time, and given their potentially serious consequences for the business it is essential that they are identified as soon as possible, preferably before they occur.

Assuming an infringement, or a potential infringement, is identified, the next role of the measurement system is to communicate that an infringement might be about to occur. Whether this is via flashing lights on control panels, statistical process control charts or a whole host of other mechanisms is unimportant at this stage. What matters is that the message comes out quickly to allow corrective action to be taken before the infringement occurs.

Once the message that action is required has been communicated, the appropriate course of action must be determined. If a nuclear reactor is about to melt down then it's probably right to shut it down. If two planes are about to collide then evasive action is what is needed. In many instances, however, the answer is not so obvious and root cause analysis has to be undertaken to identify the source of the problem.

Then, when the appropriate course of action has been confirmed, it must be compelled, that is, made to happen, stage by stage, as necessary.

The 4 CPs in check

Some of the measures used to check an organisation's health may be the same as the measures used to ensure the organisation complies with non-critical performance parameters, but the monitoring processes are likely to be different. Take the human heart, for example. Heart rate is used in two ways as a measure. When a doctor is conducting a general health check the patient's heart rate will be monitored, along with other dimensions of body performance. When, however, a patient has a cardiac arrest, a new method of monitoring heart rate is introduced and the patient is attached to a cardiogram which continually monitors heart rate. So it is with measures used to check the health of businesses. Often the measures will be reviewed monthly by the management team, but occasionally real-time, continuous monitoring processes may have to be introduced. When conducting monthly health checks the management team will be asking whether they are on track, implementing their strategy as planned, or achieving their improvement targets. Their aim is to determine whether the health of the business is likely to come under threat in the medium term.

Here the measures are being used to check the position of the business across a variety of dimensions. Once position has been checked it must be communicated, especially if corrective action is required. There are many different ways of achieving this. In its EVITA programme (pages 150–2) ABB developed a software tool consisting of three levels (see Figures 7.2a, 7.2b and 7.2c on the following pages). At the top level the aggregated information is displayed. Concerns are highlighted by arrows pointing down, showing a deterioration in performance. At the next level there is more detailed information on the subdimensions, which together make up top-level performance. Once again areas of concern are highlighted by arrows pointing down. Clicking on one of these arrows brings up the third level of analysis, the action plans, which highlight both where the organisation wants to be with regard to the dimension of performance being considered and how it plans to get there. Other organisations use traffic lights in a similar way: red for danger; amber for warning; and green to indicate no cause for concern. The aim in each case is to communicate quickly and visually whether any threats to the health of the business exist and, if so, what these threats are.

If threats to the health of the business are identified, the organisation must discuss how to counter them. Action is unlikely to be required immediately, so time for research and investigation will usually be available. Hence the task is to identify possible solutions to the problems that have been identified or to ratify solutions that have already been identified. A good example of this is provided by Rolls-Royce Aerospace's use of the Ford quality operating system visualisation (pages 62–3 and 81–3). A set of measures for assessing the health of Rolls-Royce Aerospace's procurement function was developed over a period of time by the senior managers of the function and an external facilitator. Once the measures had been documented and agreed each of the senior managers took ownership of one or more of them. At the monthly management reviews these managers were responsible for reporting progress against the measure they owned, identifying the reasons for any shortfalls in performance and proposing corrective action plans. The rest of the management team had two roles: to assess whether the action plan being proposed would adversely affect the measures they owned; and to confirm the action plans, assuming everyone agreed with them.

In the final stage of compelling progress many organisations choose to link management bonuses to performance. Whirlpool has introduced a scheme similar to the one operated by Cigna (see page 88), where every manager in Europe and every employee in Italy is paid a bonus at the

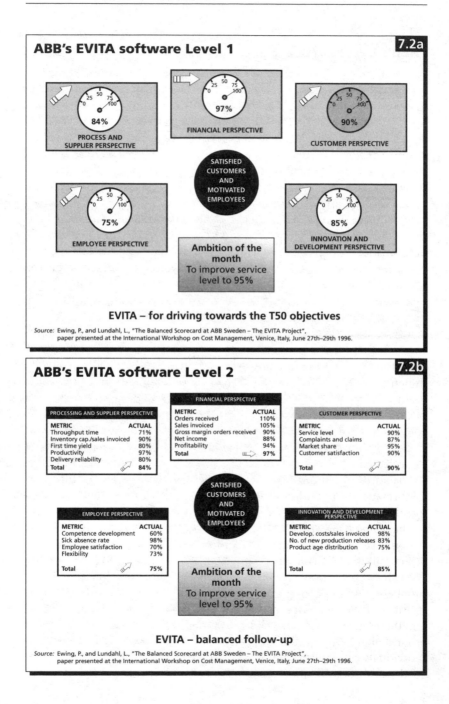

ABB's EVITA software Level 1

7.2a

PROCESS AND SUPPLIER PERSPECTIVE — 84%

FINANCIAL PERSPECTIVE — 97%

CUSTOMER PERSPECTIVE — 90%

EMPLOYEE PERSPECTIVE — 75%

SATISFIED CUSTOMERS AND MOTIVATED EMPLOYEES

INNOVATION AND DEVELOPMENT PERSPECTIVE — 85%

Ambition of the month
To improve service level to 95%

EVITA – for driving towards the T50 objectives

Source: Ewing, P., and Lundahl, L., "The Balanced Scorecard at ABB Sweden – The EVITA Project", paper presented at the International Workshop on Cost Management, Venice, Italy, June 27th–29th 1996.

ABB's EVITA software Level 2

7.2b

PROCESSING AND SUPPLIER PERSPECTIVE

METRIC	ACTUAL
Throughput time	71%
Inventory cap./sales invoiced	90%
First time yield	80%
Productivity	97%
Delivery reliability	80%
Total	**84%**

FINANCIAL PERSPECTIVE

METRIC	ACTUAL
Orders received	110%
Sales invoiced	105%
Gross margin orders received	90%
Net income	88%
Profitability	94%
Total	**97%**

CUSTOMER PERSPECTIVE

METRIC	ACTUAL
Service level	90%
Complaints and claims	87%
Market share	95%
Customer satisfaction	90%
Total	**90%**

EMPLOYEE PERSPECTIVE

METRIC	ACTUAL
Competence development	60%
Sick absence rate	98%
Employee satisfaction	70%
Flexibility	73%
Total	**75%**

SATISFIED CUSTOMERS AND MOTIVATED EMPLOYEES

INNOVATION AND DEVELOPMENT PERSPECTIVE

METRIC	ACTUAL
Develop. costs/sales invoiced	98%
No. of new production releases	83%
Product age distribution	75%
Total	**85%**

Ambition of the month
To improve service level to 95%

EVITA – balanced follow-up

Source: Ewing, P., and Lundahl, L., "The Balanced Scorecard at ABB Sweden – The EVITA Project", paper presented at the International Workshop on Cost Management, Venice, Italy, June 27th–29th 1996.

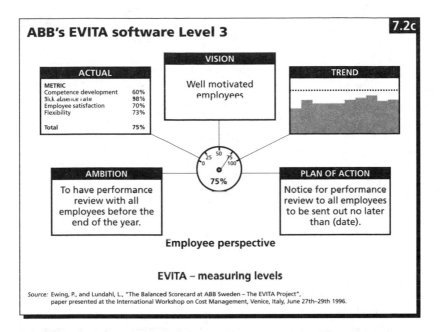

ABB's EVITA software Level 3

7.2c

VISION

Well motivated employees

ACTUAL

METRIC	
Competence development	60%
Sick absence rate	98%
Employee satisfaction	70%
Flexibility	73%
Total	75%

TREND

AMBITION

To have performance review with all employees before the end of the year.

75%

PLAN OF ACTION

Notice for performance review to all employees to be sent out no later than (date).

Employee perspective

EVITA – measuring levels

Source: Ewing, P., and Lundahl, L., "The Balanced Scorecard at ABB Sweden – The EVITA Project", paper presented at the International Workshop on Cost Management, Venice, Italy, June 27th–29th 1996.

end of the year based on performance. The bonus is calculated using two dimensions. The first is how well the business as a whole performed against its strategic targets and measures, encapsulated in Whirlpool's balanced scorecard. Performance compared with the scorecard measures is converted into a fictional share value. At the start of the year these fictional shares are valued at 100 units. At the end of the year their value is increased or decreased in accordance with Whirlpool's performance compared with its balanced scorecard. The second dimension is that of individual performance. Scorecards are also agreed for individuals. Bonuses are paid based on whether or not individuals exceed the targets on their scorecards. At the start of the year everyone is awarded a target level of Whirlpool fictional shares. This is the number of shares they will receive if they achieve all the targets on their scorecard. Those who beat their targets get extra shares, and those who miss their targets get fewer than the "target" number of shares. To calculate the bonus received by an individual member of Whirlpool the value of fictional Whirlpool shares at year-end and the number of fictional shares awarded are multiplied together. This ensures that, even if the company has a bad year, high-performing individuals can still maximise their bonuses; and if the company has a good year those who underperform are not rewarded disproportionately.

Other companies adopt different methods of compelling progress. Several, including Rolls-Royce Aerospace, name the managers responsible for specific measures. When performance against these measures is published (on display boards around the organisation), the managers responsible for enhancing performance are named. This name and shame policy sends powerful signals to managers as their reputations are on the line when it comes to specific dimensions of performance.

The 4 CPs in challenge
When measurement is used to challenge assumptions the aim is not to assess whether the strategy is being implemented right, but whether the right strategy is being implemented. To use a nautical analogy, it is not a matter of simply correcting a ship's course when it strays from the set route, it is the questioning of whether the route is the correct one to take – of challenging the assumptions that underlie the choice of route.

An organisation's strategy may be based on a linked set of assumptions, a set of beliefs about how the organisation works. It may be believed that by reducing processing times hold-ups will be reduced, and by reducing hold-ups complaints will be reduced, and by reducing complaints customer satisfaction will be increased. Perhaps, however, processing time is not the reason for hold-ups. Perhaps hold-ups exist because the layout of the operation or the processing routes are too complex. In a restaurant people may wait in line because they do not know where to sit, or do not even want to sit. Some people may prefer their meal to last longer so they can savour the atmosphere more. The critical issue is understanding what really drives business performance and that understanding can only be properly arrived at once the assumptions about performance have been tested and challenged. Many managers claim – largely on the basis of gut feelings – that they know what makes their business tick, but few actually exploit the power of the performance data to which they have access.

In the challenge process the first CP, checking position, involves using the measures to check the validity of the strategy. Performance data can be used to assess which of the assumptions underpinning the strategy are valid and which are not, and to identify the real drivers of customer and employee satisfaction, rapid throughput and high levels of efficiency. The data allow models of this business to be built, which can be used to make predictions about whether the right strategy is being pursued and whether the right initiatives and action plans are in place. Once built, these models have to be communicated and debated. Through this process new priorities can be confirmed and progress compelled.

Consider the time waves

The best way to distinguish between the three roles of measurement is to consider them as the different time waves that underpin the organisation's activities. Without an appropriate means of ensuring compliance, which should involve a continuous process, the organisation could die in the short term, because it could quite simply lose its licence to operate. Without appropriate health checks the organisation could die in the short to medium term, just by withering away. Without an appropriate challenge process the organisation could die in the medium to long term, because it will simply be doing the wrong things. At one level these processes undoubtedly exist in organisations today. Managers keep an eye on critical variables. They revisit their strategies and debate their validity. What is missing, however, is the recognition that the data many organisations are already collecting could be used to facilitate and enrich these processes. The world being suggested is not one where gut feelings, opinion and observation are discarded, but one where they are supplemented by appropriate performance data.

Making the most of your measurement system

Are you maximising the benefits you derive from your organisation's measurement systems? Do you use the data you have access to as a means of ensuring compliance, checking health and challenging assumptions? To help answer these questions this final section presents a matrix which builds upon the ideas presented in this book and which allows managers to assess the maturity of measurement practices within their own organisations. It consists of three dimensions. The first reflects the maturity of measurement practice and runs from novice through to master. The second emphasises the benefits of measurement, in terms of its ability to allow managers to check position (CP1), communicate position (CP2), confirm priorities (CP3) and compel progress (CP4). The third recognises the different roles that measurement systems play in organisations – ensuring compliance with non-negotiable performance parameters, allowing the health of a business to be checked, and providing data which can be used to challenge the assumptions that underlie an organisation's strategy. Take, for example, checking health. At the level of the novice, an organisation would have unstructured health assessment processes. It would probably focus on financial measures, occasionally surveying customers and employees. Little effort would have been made to link the measures to the organisation's strategy. At the level of master, however, health would be checked regularly through a comprehensive review of a balanced set of measures. The links between the measures and the organisation's strategy would be obvious. Display boards, visual indicators and comprehensive information systems (possibly intranets) would be used to communicate the relevant information throughout the organisation.

Figures 7.3–7.5 on the following pages summarise the arguments for each of the three roles of measurement and provide a useful means of auditing whether a given organisation is making the most of its measurement systems. The way to do this is to ask a sample of people within the organisation to assess the maturity of its measurement practices using the scales provided. If they think that the statement "Limited performance data communicated through the organisation. That which is tends to be too little, too late." most accurately describes the organisation's approach they would score their business a novice in terms of check health, communicate position. If, however, they think the statement "Results of performance review process widely communicated. Extensive use of visual indicators, display boards and appropriate information systems (eg intranets)." is more accurate they would score their organisation master in terms of check health, communicate position. Scores of master are worth 4 points on the scale, and scores of novice are worth 1. The assessment can be repeated for each of the four CPS, for each role of measurement (comply, check and challenge). The resultant data can be plotted on the polar chart shown in Figure 7.6 on page 194, which clearly highlights where the organisation's measurement systems are strong and where they are weak.

The challenge for the future

Criticism of traditional financially based measures is widespread. Numerous frameworks and alternative methods of measurement designed to overcome their weaknesses have been devised. This book has explained and explored the most valuable of these, and has shown how a number of companies have adapted them for their own use. Most importantly, the book has also explored the notion that measurement plays a variety of roles in organisations. Sometimes it is used to help ensure compliance with an organisation's non-negotiable performance parameters – the performance threshold on which its licence to operate effectively depends. Sometimes it is used as a means of checking an

Measures as a means of ensuring compliance

7.3

	NOVICE	AMATEUR	PROFESSIONAL	MASTER
CHECK POSITION	Non-negotiable performance parameters not identified. No explicit measures for non-negotiable performance parameters available.	Non-negotiable performance parameters recognised. Some relevant measures available but generally they are historical in nature.	Most non-negotiable performance parameters identified. Relevant measures generally available, some of which are predictive.	Non-negotiable performance parameters recognised and clearly defined. Predictive measures available for most non-negotiable performance parameters.
COMMUNICATE POSITION	No early warning systems in place. Infringements identified only after the event and often by external parties.	Infringements generally identified after the event, although usually identified internally.	Early-warning systems in place for some non-negotiable parameters. Hence potential infringements sometimes identified in advance.	Early-warning systems in place for all non-negotiable performance parameters. Potential infringements almost always identified in advance.
CONFIRM PRIORITIES	Infringements dealt with reactively – usually in crisis management mode.	Clear contingency plans in place to deal with infringements as and when they occur. Emphasis on systems and procedures to try and prevent infringements occurring.	Some potential infringements are dealt with in advance. Others are dealt with rapidly once they have come to light.	Pro-active early-warning systems mean that almost all infringements are dealt with in advance.
COMPEL PROGRESS	No clear roles and responsibilities for managing performance versus non-negotiable performance parameters.	Limited clarity as to who manages performance versus non-negotiable performance parameters. Generally seen as part of someone's job.	General awareness of who is responsible for managing performance versus non-negotiable performance parameters.	Named individuals responsible for each of the non-negotiable performance parameters. Clear roles, expectations and sanctions.

7.4

Measures as a means of checking health

	NOVICE	AMATEUR	PROFESSIONAL	MASTER
CHECK POSITION	Health rarely checked even when emphasis is placed on financial measures. Surveys of customers and employees are infrequent and ad hoc.	Health checked through a review of financial and non-financial measures. Typical measures considered include the financials and customer and employee satisfaction.	Health checked at regular intervals using a balanced set of measures. How the measures map on to the organisation's strategy is not immediately obvious.	Health checked through regular review of balanced set of measures which truly reflect the organisation's strategic imperatives.
COMMUNICATE POSITION	Limited performance data communicated through the organisation. That which is tends to be too little, too late.	Communication of current position via internal newsletters and some display boards. Often the information is comparatively old by the time it sees the light of day.	Results of performance review communicated. Display boards and visual indicators used in most parts of the organisation.	Results of performance review process widely communicated. Extensive use of visual indicators, display boards and appropriate information systems (eg, intranets).
CONFIRM PRIORITIES	Actions plans are developed, but usually on the basis of gut feel rather than a systematic process.	Actions are identified through performance review process, although many of those proposed are not explicitly related to performance data being reviewed.	Performance review process generally results in actions being proposed, although not all actions are as well thought through as they should be.	Performance review process concentrates on priorities and action plans. Discussion centres on how to overcome performance shortfalls, not just the reasons for shortfalls.
COMPEL PROGRESS	Few of the action plans that are developed are implemented. Even fewer result in tangible business benefits.	A significant number of the actions identified during the review process are not followed up. Others are partially implemented, although often on an ad hoc basis.	Follow-up of actions proposed at review is reasonable, although some action plans fall by the wayside as other priorities take over.	Actions to be taken following review widely communicated. Explicit links between action plans and organisation's incentive and penalty schemes.

7.5

Measures as a means of challenging assumptions

	NOVICE	AMATEUR	PROFESSIONAL	MASTER
CHECK POSITION	Assumptions underpinning strategy not understood. In fact notion of strategy as a set of linked assumptions not understood.	Assumptions underpinning strategy recognised, but not widely understood. Different people have different views of what the strategy involves.	Assumptions underpinning strategy recognised and sometimes challenged, although usually on the basis of gut feel rather than facts and figures.	Assumptions underpinning strategy clearly stated and regularly tested. Gut feel supplemented by hard facts and figures.
COMMUNICATE POSITION	Lack of clarity in theory of business and associated assumptions means that few understand in depth where the organisation is going or how it is going to get there.	Some debate about where the organisation is and where it is going, but little agreement. Debate happens once a year and then is forgotten until the following year.	Senior management involved in debate about strategic direction and aware of changes. Others employees told rather than involved.	Theory of business clearly stated and widely understood by all within organisation. Everyone invited to critique theory and suggest ways in which it can be improved.
CONFIRM PRIORITIES	Strategy rarely changed, except in times of crisis. No obvious forum for questioning the basis or validity of the organisation's strategy.	Strategy changed occasionally. Usually as a result of annual away-days, or because of external intervention.	Strategy changed when necessary, although usually later than it should have been. Most changes based on gut feel and general information.	Changes in assumptions and hence subsequent changes in strategy clearly articulated. Rational basis for decisions, including some hard evidence or data.
COMPEL PROGRESS	Measurement and reward systems static. Both are rarely changed and now bear little resemblance to organisation's strategy.	Senior managers' reward systems linked to strategy. Link between organisation's measures and strategy less obvious.	Measurement and reward systems generally consistent with strategy, although they often do not catch up immediately; ie, strategy changes and measurement and reward systems follow.	Changes in direction clearly communicated. Measurement and reward systems always updated to reflect revised strategic direction.

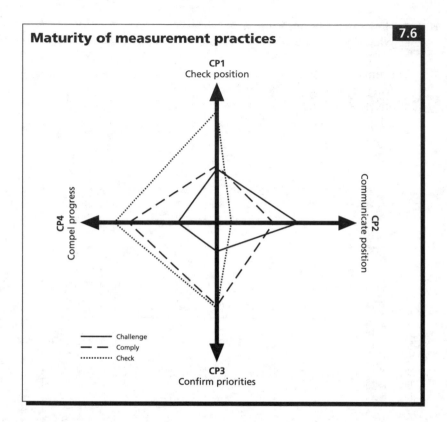

Maturity of measurement practices 7.6

organisation's health, because the data generated through the measurement system enable managers to answer the question: Is our strategy being implemented as planned? Sometimes the data provided by the measurement system are used to challenge the assumptions behind an organisation's strategy, thereby allowing managers to answer the question: Is the strategy we are implementing the right one?

In these days of ever increasing competitiveness and constantly evolving markets, the way a business performs is crucial to its success – and indeed its survival. For organisations and the people who work for them, the challenges inherent in developing and implementing robust measurement systems can be encapsulated in the following four questions:

- ◪ Why do we want to measure our performance?
- ◪ What do we measure and what should we measure?

- How should we measure these things?
- What should we do with the data once we have them?

The aim of this book has been to challenge the way people think about measuring business performance and to encourage them to think perceptively about it. In doing so, the ideas and concepts presented here should help them find answers to these crucial questions.

Notes

Introduction

1 Kaplan, R.S. and Norton, D. P., *The Balanced Scorecard – Translating Strategy into Action*, Harvard Business School Press, Boston, MA, 1996.

2 Rappaport, A., *Creating Shareholder Value: The New Standard for Business Performance*, Free Press, New York, 1998.

Chapter 1

1 Slack, N., *The Manufacturing Advantage: Achieving Competitive Manufacturing Operations*, Mercury, London, 1991.

2 Eccles, R.G., "The Performance Measurement Manifesto", *Harvard Business Review*, January–February, 1991, pp. 131–137.

3 David Norton, "Creating Future Value with the Balanced Business Scorecard", keynote address at Business Intelligence conference, London, February 1997.

4 Mavrinac, S., and Siesfeld, T., "Measures That Matter: An Exploratory Investigation of Investors' Information Needs and Value Priorities", Richard Ivey School of Business Working Paper, January 1997.

5 Philips, M., Sadler, P., and Edington, D., *The Inclusive Approach and Business Success: The Research Evidence*, second draft, Centre for Tomorrow's Company, London, 1997.

6 Ibid.

7 UK government white paper on Competitiveness, quoting RSA *Tomorrow's Company* Inquiry Report, May 1994.

8 Foundation of Manufacturing Committee of the National Academy of Engineering, United States.

9 Jones, O.T., and Sasser, W.E., "Why Satisfied Customers Defect", *Harvard Business Review*, Vol. 73, No. 6, 1995.

10 Reichheld, F.F., and Sasser, W.E., "Zero Defections: Quality Comes to Services", *Harvard Business Review*, September–October, 1990.

11 Heskett, J.L., Jones, T.O., Loveman, G.W., Sasser, W.E., and Schlesinger, L.A., "Putting the Service-Profit Chain to Work", *Harvard Business Review*, March–April, 1994.

12 Reichheld, F.F., and Sasser, W.E., "Zero Defections: Quality Comes to Services", *Harvard Business Review*, September–October, 1990.

13 Stone, C.L., "A Model to Facilitate the Use of Soft Employee-Related

Measures in the Analysis of Business Performance", unpublished PhD thesis, Anglia Polytechnic University, May 1997.

14 Patterson, M., West, M., Lawthom, R., and Nickell, S., "Do Employee Attitudes Predict Company Performance?", FMI Brief, November 1997.

15 Caulkin, S., "How that Pat on the Head Can Mean Money in the Bank", *The Observer*, April 19th 1998.

16 Ashton, C., *Strategic Performance Measurement*, Business Intelligence, London, 1997.

17 McConnachie, G., "Dow's Quest for Intellectual Value", *Measuring Business Excellence*, Vol. 1, No. 2, 1997, pp. 18–22.

18 Ibid.

19 Edvinsson, L., "Developing Intellectual Capital at Skandia", *Long Range Planning*, Vol. 30, No. 3, 1997, pp. 366–373.

20 Ashton, C., *Strategic Performance Measurement*, Business Intelligence, London, 1997.

21 *Tomorrow's Company: The Role of Business in a Changing World*, Royal Society of Arts, London, 1995.

22 Ibid.

23 Coleman, I., and Eccles, R., *Pursuing Value: Reporting Gaps in the United Kingdom*, PricewaterhouseCoopers, 1997.

24 Blitz, A., Siesfeld, T., and Bierbusse, P., *Measures that Matter*, Ernst & Young Centre for Business Innovation, Boston, 1997.

Chapter 2

1 Johnson, T., and Jakeman, M., *The Customer Challenge – The Inside Story of a Remarkable Transformation in Customer Service*, Pitman, 1997.

2 *Corporate Governance: Performance Measurement in the Digital Age*, Institute of Chartered Accountants in England and Wales, January 1998.

3 Dixon, J.R., Nanni, A.J., and Vollmann, T.E., *The New Performance Challenge – Measuring Operations for World-Class Competition*, Dow Jones-Irwin, Homewood, IL, 1990.

4 Jeanes, C., "Customer Satisfaction and Business Results: Is There a Link?", *Customer Services Management*, March 1996, pp. 46–48.

5 Johnson, T., and Jakeman, M., op. cit.

6 Neely, A.D., Mills, J.F., Platts, K.W., Gregory, M.J., and Richards, A.H., "Realising Strategy through Measurement", *International Journal of Operations and Production Management*, Vol. 14, No. 3, 1994, pp. 140–152.

7   Dixon, J.R., Nanni, A.J., and Vollmann, T.E., op. cit.

8   Thanks are due to my two colleagues, Mike Kennerley and Dan Waggoner, who conducted the study reported here.

9   Kaplan, R.S., "The Evolution of Management Accounting", *The Accounting Review*, Vol. 59, No. 3, 1984, pp. 390–418.

10 Kaplan, R.S., "Measuring Manufacturing Performance – A New Challenge for Managerial Accounting Research", *The Accounting Review*, Vol. 58, No. 4, 1983, pp. 686–705.

11 Schemenner, R.W., "Escaping the Black Holes of Cost Accounting", *Business Horizons*, January–February 1988, pp. 66–72.

12 Cooper, R., "The Two-Stage Procedure in Cost Accounting: Part 1", *Journal of Cost Management*, Summer 1987a, pp. 43–51; Cooper, R., "The Two-Stage Procedure in Cost Accounting: Part 2", *Journal of Cost Management*, Fall 1987b, pp. 39–45.

13 Galloway, D., and Waldron, D., "Throughput Accounting Part 1 – The Need for a New Language for Manufacturing", *Management Accounting*, November 1988a, pp. 34–35; Galloway, D., and Waldron, D., "Throughput Accounting Part 2 – Ranking Products Profitability", *Management Accounting*, December 1988b, pp. 34–35; Galloway, D., and Waldron, D., "Throughput Accounting Part 3 – A Better Way to Control Labour Costs", *Management Accounting*, January 1989a, pp. 32–33; Galloway, D., and Waldron, D., "Throughput Accounting Part 4 – Moving on to Complex Products", *Management Accounting*, February 1989b, pp. 40–41.

14 Johnson, H.T., and Kaplan, R.S., *Relevance Lost – The Rise and Fall of Management Accounting*, Harvard Business School Press, Boston, MA, 1987.

15 Mintzberg, H., "Patterns in Strategy Formulation", *Management Science*, Vol. 24, No. 9, 1978, pp. 934–948.

16 Camp, R.C., *Benchmarking – The Search for Industry Best Practices that Lead to Superior Performance*, ASQS Quality Press, Milwaukee, WI, 1989.

17 Andersen Consulting, *The Lean Enterprise Benchmarking Project*, London, February 1993; Andersen Consulting, *Worldwide Manufacturing Competitiveness Study – The Second Lean Enterprise Report*, London, 1994; Andersen Consulting, *Inside the Chinese Automotive Industry – The Third Lean Enterprise Report*, London, 1998.

18 IBM Consulting and London Business School, *Made in Britain – The True State of Britain's Manufacturing Industry*, London, 1993; IBM

Consulting and London Business School, *Made in Europe – A Four Nations Best Practice Study*, London, 1994.

19 Institute of Chartered Accountants in England and Wales, op. cit.

20 Mavrinac, S., and Siesfeld, T., "Measures That Matter: An Exploratory Investigation of Investors' Information Needs and Value Priorities", Working Paper, 1997.

21 Ibid.

22 See http://www.bt.com/quality_of_service/index.htm

23 See http://www.cognos.com

24 See http://www.fpm.com

25 See http://www.valstar.co.uk

26 Meekings, A., "Unlocking the Potential of Performance Measurement: A Practical Implementation Guide", *Public Money and Management*, Vol. 15, No. 4, 1995, pp. 1–8.

27 Lingle, J.H., and Schiemann, W.A., "From Balanced Scorecard to Strategy Gauge: Is Measurement Worth It?", *Management Review*, March 1996, pp. 56–62.

28 Andersen Consulting, *Profiting from the Customer*, 1998.

29 Anderson, E.W., Fornell, C., and Lehmann, D.R., "Customer Satisfaction, Market Share, and Profitability: Findings from Sweden", *Journal of Marketing*, Vol. 58, 1994, pp. 53–66; Fornell, C., "A National Customer Satisfaction Barometer: The Swedish Experience", *Journal of Marketing*, Vol. 55, 1992, pp. 1–21.

30 Anderson, E.W., Fornell, C., and Lehmann, D.R., op. cit.

31 Ashton, C., *Strategic Performance Measurement*, Business Intelligence, London, 1997.

32 McWilliams, B., "The Measure of Success", *Across the Board*, February 1996, pp. 16–20.

Chapter 3

1   Zairi, M., *Measuring Performance for Business Results*, Chapman & Hall, London, 1994; FedEx web page (www.fedex.com).

2   *Fortune* web page (http://www.pathfinder.com/fortune/mostadmired/).

3   Andersen Consulting, *Inside the Chinese Automotive Industry: The Third Lean Enterprise Report*, London, 1994; Andersen Consulting, *The Worldwide Manufacturing Competitiveness Survey: The Second Lean Enterprise Benchmarking Report*, London, 1994.

4   Florida Power and Light web page (http://www.fpl.com).

5   Information from http://www.btrplc.com/ and through private

conversations with former BTR employees.

6   Lewis, E., "Using the Balanced Scorecard to Link Individual and Team Objectives with Overall Corporate Objectives", presentation made at the Strategic Performance Measurement Conference organised by Business Intelligence, London, 1998.

7   Kaplan, R.S., and Norton, D.P., "The Balanced Scorecard – Measures that Drive Performance, *Harvard Business Review*, January–February, 1992, pp. 71–79; Kaplan, R.S., and Norton, D.P., *The Balanced Scorecard – Translating Strategy into Action*, Harvard Business School Press, Boston, MA, 1996.

8   Zairi, M., op. cit.

9   Valerio, T., "Aligning the Organisation to the Balanced Scorecard", presentation made at the Strategic Performance Measurement Conference organised by Business Intelligence, London, 1998.

10 Simons, R., *Levers of Control: How Managers Use Innovative Control Systems to Drive Strategic Renewal*, Harvard Business School Press, Boston, MA, 1995.

Chapter 4

1   Information from proceedings of the International Chernobyl conference (http://www.iaea.or.at) and the Russian Research Centre "Kurchatov Institute" (http://polyn.net.kiae.su/polyn/manifest.html).

2   Information from Neergard, L, *New Causes for Concern about Food Contamination*, Associated Press, August 25th 1997.

3   Dwer, O., "Blood Authority Investigates Faulty Blood Bags", *British Medical Journal News*, September 1995.

4   RSA, *Tomorrow's Company: The Role of Business in a Changing World*, Royal Society of Arts, Manufacturers and Commerce, London, 1994.

5   Information from web site (http://www.marthinus.vwv.net/story2.htm).

6   Information from web site (http://www.cat.com); Tait, N., "US Workers Reject Caterpillar Deal", *Financial Times*, February 24th 1998.

7   Information from Reputation Management web site (http://www.precentral.com/RepManagement.htm).

8   Martinson, J., "Shares in the Action", *Financial Times*, April 27th 1998.

9   Information from web site (http://www.open.gov.uk/ofwat).

10 Information from web site (http://www.nortel.com).

11 Horovitz, J.H., "Strategic Control: A New Task for Top Management", *Long Range Planning*, No. 12, 1979, pp. 2–7.
12 Neave, H., *The Deming Dimension*, SPC Press, Knoxville, TN, 1990.

Chapter 5

1 Goldratt, E.M., and Cox, J., *The Goal: Beating the Competition*, Creative Output Books, Hounslow, 1986.
2 Chandler, A.D., *The Visible Hand – Managerial Revolution in American Business*, Harvard University Press, Boston, MA, 1977; Johnson, H.T., "Management Accounting in Early Integrated Industry – E.I. DuPont de Nemours Powder Company 1903–1912", *Business History Review*, Summer 1975a, pp. 184–204.
3 Reier, S., "The Man from Melbourne", FW, July 20th 1993, pp. 33–41.
4 MVA and EVA are registered trademarks of Stern Stewart, a consulting company.
5 Cooper, R., "The Rise of Activity-Based Cost Systems: Part I – What is an Activity-Based Cost System?", *Journal of Cost Management*, Summer 1988a, pp. 45–54; Cooper, R., "The Rise of Activity-Based Cost Systems: Part II – When Do I Need an Activity-Based Cost System?", *Journal of Cost Management*, Fall 1988b, pp. 41–48; Cooper, R., "The Rise of Activity-Based Cost Systems: Part III – How Many Cost Drivers Do You Need and How Should You Select Them?", *Journal of Cost Management*, Winter 1989a, pp. 34–46; Cooper, R., "The Rise of Activity-Based Cost Systems: Part IV – What Do Activity-Based Systems Look Like?", *Journal of Cost Management*, Spring 1989b, pp. 34–46.
6 Goldratt, E.M., and Cox, J., op. cit.
7 Galloway, D., and Waldron, D., "Throughput Accounting Part 1 – The Need for a New Language for Manufacturing", *Management Accounting*, November 1988a, pp. 34–35; Galloway, D., and Waldron, D., "Throughput Accounting Part 2 – Ranking Products Profitability", *Management Accounting*, December 1988b, pp. 34–35; Galloway, D., and Waldron, D., "Throughput Accounting Part 3 – A Better Way to Control Labour Costs", *Management Accounting*, January 1989a, pp. 32–33; Galloway, D., and Waldron, D., "Throughput Accounting Part 4 – Moving on to Complex Products", *Management Accounting*, February 1989b, pp. 40–41.
8 Rappaport, A., *Creating Shareholder Value: The New Standard for Business Performance*, Free Press, New York, 1998; Stewart, G. B., *The Quest for Value: The EVA Management Guide*, HarperBusiness, New

York, 1991.

9   Information from Stern Stewart web site (http://www.sternstewart.com).

10 *Fortune Magazine*, September 9th 1996.

11 Information from Stern Stewart web site (http://www.sternstewart.com).

12 Ibid.

13 Slack, N., *The Manufacturing Advantage: Achieving Competitive Manufacturing Operations*, Mercury, London, 1991.

14 Hill, T., *Manufacturing Strategy: The Strategic Management of the Manufacturing Function*, Macmillan, Basingstoke, 1993.

15 Steeples, M.M., *The Corporate Guide to the Malcolm Baldridge National Quality Award*, ASQC Quality Press, Milwaukee, WI, 1993; National Institute of Standards and Technology home page (www.NIST.quality.gov).

16 National Institute of Standards and Technology home page (www.NIST.quality.gov).

17 Garvin, D.A., "How the Baldridge Award Really Works", *Harvard Business Review*, November–December, 1991.

18 Anonymous, Raytheon (www.raytheon.com).

19 Information from EQFM home page (http://www.efqm.org).

20 Crosby, P., *Quality is Free*, New American Library, New York, 1980.

21 Hayes, R.H.; Wheelwright, S.C., and Clark, K.B., *Dynamic Manufacturing: Creating the Learning Organisation*, Free Press, New York, 1988.

22 Kaplan, R.S., and Norton, D.P., "The Balanced Scorecard – Measures that Drive Performance", *Harvard Business Review*, January–February, 1992, pp. 71–79; Kaplan, R.S., and Norton, D.P., *The Balanced Scorecard – Translating Strategy into Action*, Harvard Business School Press, Boston, MA, 1996.

23 Brown, M., *Keeping Score: Using the Right Metrics to Drive World Class Performance*, Quality Resources, New York, 1996.

24 Meryl Bushell, Head of Customer Service Development and Customer Measures for BT, speaking at BI Conference, London, February 1997.

25 Ibid.

Chapter 6

1   De Geus, A., "Companies: What Are They?", lecture to the RSA on January 25th 1995.

2   Porter, M., *Competitive Strategy: Techniques for Analyzing Industries and Competitors*, Free Press, New York, 1980.

3   Prahalad, C.K., and Hamel, G., "The Core Competence of the Corporation", *Harvard Business Review*, May–June 1990, pp. 79–91.

4   Drucker, P., The Emerging Theory of Manufacturing, *Harvard Business Review*, May–June 1990.

5   Jeanes, C., "Customer Satisfaction and Business Results: Is There a Link?", *Customer Services Management*, March 1996, pp. 46–48.

6   Ibid.

7   Meekings, A., "Unlocking the Potential of Performance Measurement: A Practical Implementation Guide", *Public Money and Management*, Vol. 15, No. 4, 1995, pp. 1–8.

8   Rucci, A.J., Kim, S.P., and Quinn, R.T., "The Employee-Customer Profit Chain at Sears", *Harvard Business Review*, January–February 1998, pp. 83–97.

9   Meryl Bushell, head of customer service development and customer measures for BT, speaking at BI Conference, London, February 1997.

10 Thanks are due to my colleague Mohammed Al-Najjar, who conducted the research described in this case study.

Chapter 7

1   Information from Reuters Report, December 3rd 1994; EarthBase (www.earthbase.org); Reputation Management (www.prcentral.com/RepManagement.htm).

2   Kaplan, R.S., and Norton, D.P., "The Balanced Scorecard – Measures that Drive Performance, *Harvard Business Review*", January–February 1992, pp. 71–79; Kaplan, R.S., and Norton, D.P., *The Balanced Scorecard – Translating Strategy into Action*, Harvard Business School Press, Boston, MA, 1996.

3   Eccles, R.G., and Pyburn, P.J., "Creating a Comprehensive System to Measure Performance", *Management Accounting* (US), October 1992, pp. 41–44.

4   Argyris, C., and Schön, D., *Organisational Learning: A Theory of Action Perspective*, Addison-Wesley, Reading, 1978.

List of companies referred to